To
Masayuki Suzuki
Best regards.
Susan F. Semel
1997
March 27,

The Dalton School

American University Studies

Series XIV
Education

Vol. 34

PETER LANG
New York • San Francisco • Bern • Baltimore
Frankfurt am Main • Berlin • Wien • Paris

Susan F. Semel

The Dalton School

The Transformation of a Progressive School

PETER LANG
New York • San Francisco • Bern • Baltimore
Frankfurt am Main • Berlin • Wien • Paris

Library of Congress Cataloging-in-Publication Data

Semel, Susan F.
  The Dalton School : the transformation of a progressive school /
Susan F. Semel.
    p. cm. — (American university studies. Series XIV, Education ;
vol. 34)
  Includes bibliographical references (p.   ).
  1. Dalton School (New York, N.Y.)—History. I. Title. II. Series.
LD7501.N495S44   1992   373.747'1—dc20   91-3819
ISBN 0-8204-2208-8 (hbk)   CIP
ISBN 0-8204-1482-4 (pbk)
ISSN 0740-4565

Die Deutsche Bibliothek-CIP-Einheitsaufnahme

Semel, Susan F.:
The Dalton School : the transformation of a progressive school / Susan
F. Semel.—New York; Berlin, Bern; Frankfurt/M.; Paris; Wien; Lang, 1992
  (American university studies : Ser. 14, Education ; Vol. 34)
    ISBN 0-8204-1482-4
NE: American university studies / 14

"Gift of a Great Teacher," by Fred Hechinger, copyright © 1987 by
The New York Times Company. Reprinted by permission.

Cover Design by George Lallas.

Front cover photo by Douglass Ridgeway.

The paper in this book meets the guidelines for permanence and
durability of the Committee on Production Guidelines for
Book Longevity of the Council on Library Resources.

© Peter Lang Publishing, Inc., New York 1992

Printed in the United States of America.

To my mother, Lucille Fleschner and
To the memory of my father, Cecil Fleschner

who had the good sense to send me to Dalton

and

To the memory of Lawrence A. Cremin

who encouraged me to write its history

ACKNOWLEDGEMENTS

This book would not have been possible without the assistance of a number of caring and helpful colleagues and friends. My dissertation committee at Teachers College, Columbia University, provided essential commentary, guidance, and criticism on what were first drafts of Chapters 2-5 and parts of Chapter 6 and Chapter 8 of this book. The late Lawrence A. Cremin, Maxine Greene, and Francis Ianni all provided exemplary support. Diane Ravitch, who was an outside reader, also provided helpful assistance and comments.

Early research for this book was made possible by a Klingenstein Fellowship at Teachers College. My year as a fellow allowed me to interact with a group of talented, dedicated, and thoughtful independent school educators. It was during my year in residence as a fellow, 1978-1979, that I began this project. I hope that this book will provide future Klingenstein fellows with food for thought about independent school leadership.

At Dalton, Marilyn Moss (formerly Feldman), Gardner Dunnan, Frank Moretti, Frank Carnabuci, Susan Etess, Connie Mayer, Stanley Seidman, David Arnold, Cameron Hendershot, and Janet Pertusi provided essential assistance in my research. Marilyn Moss was helpful in helping me with archival research. I want to thank especially Gardner Dunnan for providing me with access to the Dalton archives and for his willingness to talk to me at length about his years as Headmaster. Frank Carnabuci, Stanley Seidman, Susan Etess, Connie Mayer and Frank Moretti also gave generously of their time and talked to me at length. Also, faculty, students, and parents too numerous to mention generously shared their experiences. In particular, former students of mine David Cremin and Jamie Gangel spent long hours reminiscing about Dalton, when I visited with them respectively in San Francisco in 1989 and Washington D.C. in 1990 during the Annual Meetings of the American Sociological Association.

A number of colleagues have read part or all of the book. These include Nick Aversa, Linda Bunting, Peter W. Cookson, Jr., Diana Feige, Sharon Fougner, Maxine Greene, Martin Haas, Kathe Jervis, David Levinson, Carl Rheins, Alan R. Sadovnik, Pierre Woog and Ed Yeomans. Their comments and suggestions have been invaluable. Kathe Jervis, David Levinson, and Ed Yeomans provided detailed and helpful comments on the first draft of the manuscript. Peter W. Cookson, Jr., a former Dalton student, provided insight into the Dalton of his youth. Alan R. Sadovnik provided especially important sociological insights and kept me honest, by reminding me of the progressive paradox of elite education at the Dalton School. My son, John, a former student at Dalton also made valuable comments on the manuscript. Sharon Fougner copy edited the entire manuscript, as did my editor at Peter Lang, Heidi Burns. I would like to thank Heidi Burns for all of her support and help from the acquisitions stage to final production. Additionally, Kathy Iwasaki, Christine Marra, Michael Flamini and Chris Myers at Peter Lang were invaluable during the final stages of production.

This book would not have been possible without the secretarial and computer support provided at Adelphi University. Janet Murphy typed the original manuscript into the word processor. Martha Meyer provided helpful computer assistance. Brian Helman and especially Danielle Daum of the Adelphi Computer Center provided exceptional computer support, without which this book could not have been completed. Linda DeVries, my graduate student in the history of education, provided outstanding typing, computer and editorial assistance. Alan R. Sadovnik helped me to master the ins and outs of preparing the manuscript.

Although I did not write about students specifically in this book, I would be remiss if I did not acknowledge all of the wonderful and special students I taught during my years at Dalton. They were creative, articulate, often idiosynchratic, often brilliant and talented, and made teaching a joy. Likewise, my colleagues over the years made working at Dalton worthwhile and they defined professionalism.

My family has endured the trials and tribulations of this project. I thank them for their patience and understanding.

I have dedicated this book to my late father and my mother, who had the good sense to send me to Dalton. I wish my father had lived to read this book. My mother, Lucille Fleschner, worked selflessly for over twenty years as the volunteer chair of the Dalton Thrift Shop. She has been a member of the Dalton community for over a quarter of a century and has exemplified the meaning of community spirit so much a part of the school's tradition.

Finally, I have dedicated this book to my mentor, the late Lawrence A. Cremin. In addition to being a model to which historians of education aspire, Lawrence A. Cremin had a monumental influence on my life. As my teacher, mentor, and Dalton parent, he encouraged me to write the history of the Dalton School and guided the dissertation to its completion. Unfortunately, his untimely death prevents him from seeing the final product, this book. Nonetheless, his influence on this work is everywhere. Historians of education will recognize that the subtitle of this book, *The Transformation of a Progressive School*, pays homage to his groundbreaking book on progressive education.

TABLE OF CONTENTS

FOREWORD

At a moment when the school restructuring movement is infused with ideas and values recalling the work of John Dewey, the story of the Dalton School is of startling interest. Associated from the beginning with "progressive education," Dalton has moved through phases of advancement and decline that have in many ways reflected what has happened in American education and in the culture at large.

Susan Semel tells the story by tracing the lives and careers of the School's headmistresses and headmasters, beginning with the celebrated Helen Parkhurst, its founder. Because she is a historian, the author is able to locate each one in time and context. Each one's tale, therefore, becomes a mini-drama of transaction between a particular personality and a particular vision of society. The conceptions of education that result, therefore, are contingent on character, orientation, and commitment. Class loyalties, pragmatic considerations, financial demands all enter in; and readers cannot but become engaged in identifying causal factors, envisaging alternative possibilities, trying to account for the past and present significance of the Dalton School.

Dr. Semel presents her work as a qualitative study; and she is indeed a privileged participant and observer. Alumna, parent, social studies teacher, and eventually researcher, she is able to look through multiple perspectives at a "reality" never susceptible to one-dimensional definition. Her distinctive voice becomes reflective at times, critical at times, simply interrogative at other times. It becomes a voice in a chorus of voices at various intervals, since Dr. Semel has consulted and personally interviewed numbers of persons connected in diverse ways to the institution: Board members; administrators; teachers; students; every one of whom speaks in a different tone. She has consulted a number of nationally known academics as well and read the works of significant participants, ranging from Ralph Tyler to Lawrence Cremin. Her bibliography has expanded around these works; until, when the book is done, the story reaches far beyond an account of an urban, middle class, private school renowned in popular culture as much as in the academic realm.

Burning curriculum questions having to do with the "canon," with tradition, with lived experience are opened as the book proceeds. So are questions having to do with bureaucracies, large and small, with modes of organization and supervision in public as well as private schools. Most interesting, perhaps, are the questions having to do with the ways in which schools respond—and ought to respond—to the offerings, promises, and temptations held out by private groups, ignoble or noble, or both.

Dr. Semel has not spent her time merely examining and interpreting a problematic past. She has developed a fascinating history of a school that has become part of the folklore of middle-class, intellectual New York City as it has changed in the past seventy years. She has stimulated readers to pose questions that must be posed if the Deweyan tradition is to be properly evaluated and understood, and if its future (perhaps in still unpredictable forms) is to be assured. This book is a new beginning in a wide-ranging account of 20th century "progressive" schools. It is a beginning well worth sampling by those who realize that the most significant historical questions are those hitherto unsolved.

Maxine Greene
Teachers College
Columbia University

PREFACE

My association with the Dalton School has spanned over a quarter of a century, as a student, teacher, parent, and researcher. I attended Dalton as a student during Charlotte Durham's administration. I returned to teach social studies during Donald Barr's administration and continued as a teacher through Gardner Dunnan's administration until 1988, when I joined the faculty at Adelphi University as an Assistant Professor of Education.

I have also been a Dalton parent. My son, John, attended Dalton from kindergarten through grade eight, during Gardner Dunnan's administration.

In the course of my years at Dalton, I have personally known three of its heads and two of its interim heads. Many of the faculty members I write of have either taught me or have been my colleagues. Many children I have taught have been offspring of former schoolmates. Many of the events I have described I have witnessed firsthand. Thus, I have approached my subject with my own special history, my own personal landscape. Given this subjective landscape, I have worked diligently at bracketing out my personal experiences and have attempted to analyze the history of the school as an historian of education. Nevertheless, writing the history of a school in which one has been so intimately involved poses significant methodological concerns.

This book began in 1978, when as a Klingenstein Fellow at Teachers College, Columbia University I began to research the history of the Dalton School for my doctoral dissertation. My dissertation, completed in 1984, under the mentorship of Lawrence A. Cremin, examined the history of the school through the Barr administration. As I still was a member of the Dalton faculty, Professor Cremin and I agreed that the dissertation would not include the Dunnan years, for obvious pragmatic considerations. When I left Dalton in 1988, I decided to turn the dissertation into a book by completing the history through the Dunnan administration. What I thought at first glance would require looking only at these years, ultimately required a recasting of the original material. Thus, in addition to a new chapter on Dunnan, and new introductory and concluding chapters, there are new additions to the chapter on Barr and a new Epilogue. Additionally, I discovered that I could not simply begin to write the history of the Dunnan years without first sufficiently distancing myself from the events in which I was so intimately involved. The process of bracketing out my own experiences discussed above proved to be significantly more challenging for the period closest to my writing. As an historian it was essential to have sufficient time lapse between the events and their analysis. Thus, although I began to think about returning to this history in 1988, I did not begin the research for this book until 1990, when I felt I had gained the requisite objectivity necessary to write solid history.

Although my research does not constitute participant observational field research in the strict sense as practiced by anthropologists and sociologists as I did not conduct research as a participant, I am cognizant that many of the problems of participant observation as a participant are applicable to my research. Whereas participant observers are involved in the organization that they are studying as they are conducting their research, I was a part of the organization that I looked at historically. Nonetheless, the problem of "going native", a central issue in field research, presented an interesting dilemma, since to some extent I have always been native. Thus, I constantly had to examine my own perceptions of the history of the school as a participant in that history and compare it to other evidence, such as archival documents and interviews. Sometimes my perceptions as a member coincided with other sources; sometimes they varied. As an historian I had to treat my own perceptions as just another piece of evidence and then I had to make sense of any contradictions. This required a type of psychoanalytic journey, one which most historians do not need to take so explicitly in their work. Suffice it to say that at times this was difficult; so much so that when I began to research the Dunnan years, I realized that I needed some time before I could separate my feelings as a participant from my role as an historian. Through constant self-examination, reflection, criticism, and ongoing discussions with colleagues both inside and outside of Dalton, I am confident that I have confronted the problems associated with this type of research. My awareness of the possibility of researcher bias kept me honest and I have tried to be as objective as anyone doing history. Since complete objectivity is a myth of positivism, I believe that I have kept within the boundaries of writing good history.

The sociologist, Jack Douglas, in *Investigative Social Research*, analyzes the problems associated with investigative field research. In his discussion of research based upon direct experience as a member he outlines the major criticisms of in-depth involvement and concludes that despite problems of possible researcher bias, the experienced researcher, through careful and constant self-reflection, can overcome these dilemmas and in doing so gain important insights impossible under other, less involved circumstances. In the same vein, writing history as a participant (and former participant), while posing serious challenges, provided a perspective that a non-participant might never have achieved.

My position as a participant and historian posed some ethical dilemmas. The most important problem concerned the use of information given to me as a participant, when I was teaching at Dalton, rather than as an historian writing about the school. Since I participated in the school for over 25 years, I was witness to events that most historians would never have witnessed first hand. More importantly, the question of whether to include information offered to me in my role as a participant, not as a researcher, presented the most serious ethical dilemma. Although I have based my analysis on both information given to me in both roles, the book does not reproduce private conversations that were told to me as a participant. Further, I have attempted to coroborate important historical data with at least two sources.

A word must be said about the historical sources used in my research. I have relied on interviews and conversations with administrators, faculty, students, alumni, parents, and board members. In both instances the individuals were informed of my research project. Some individuals specifically agreed to talk to me on the condition that they were granted anonymity. Therefore, I often attribute information and quotes to informants. In the case of formal interviews, where the individual agreed to be identified, I have included this information in the footnotes. In no case, have I quoted anyone who did not make a statement with full knowledge of the research. Therefore, I never quoted, even anonomously, anyone who said something to me in my other roles as teacher or parent. Finally, in no instance did I quote anyone who spoke to me as a participant, but not as a researcher, with the exception of statements made at public settings. In these cases, I have for the most part not referred to individuals by name, with the exception of the major figures in the school's history: its heads.

The Dalton archives provided significant data for the study, albeit spotty. There were few archival records for the early years, and spotty records for the Barr years. Only the Dunnan years proved a treasure trove of archival material and this is reflected in the increased use of documentary sources for the Dunnan chapter. As well, many documents from the Dunnan years are in my possession since as an alumna, parent, and former faculty member, I was the recipient of numerous pamphlets, newsletters, newspapers, and annual reports. Thus, for the Dunnan years, unless noted as specifically in the archives, all documents quoted are in the author's possession.

Thus, although there are problems with writing history as a former participant, what is important is that I have consciously removed myself in the writing of the school's history from my actions as a former participant. The result, I believe, is a study that is informed both by the subjective understanding of an insider and the historical insight of an outsider. Although this was not easy, Douglas' conclusions about in-depth direct experience support its validity as a form of social and historical investigation.

In conclusion, I need to say something about the book I did write and the ones that I consciously chose not to write. This book examines the transformation of a school founded in the progressive tradition, from its inception to the present. It focuses on the role of independent school leadership and school heads, in particular, in the shaping of the school's direction. Although I examine other factors, both inside and outside of the school, my principal concern was how each school head shaped and changed the school, in relation to the larger culture. This book, although it deals with progressive pedagogy, is not about curriculum and teaching practices. It does not attempt to explicitly chart the changes in teaching methods or curriculum design, nor does it make judgements as to their value; although as a progressive educator I firmly believe that many of the methods practiced at the Dalton School over the last 70 years make eminent sense today. Additionally, I have not attempted to raise policy questions concerning the relevance of progressive education in the 1990's. Although some may wish a section on "lessons from the past" and there are many, I was interested in writing school history, not in extending this history into the area of policy. Except for the Epilogue, where I examine Dalton's history in relation to progressive education, I have refrained from moving past this one historical case into the policy realm. Although there is certainly a place for such an endeavor, I did not feel this was it. Questions of pedagogy and policy are important and to treat these issues well would have taken another book.

Moreover, such pedagogical and policy questions may best be discussed in a broader historical context, and to do this, one must look at more than one case. What is called for are more histories of progressive schools in order to understand why some survived, while others failed to survive and how their progressive practices relate to current educational concerns. Currently, I am beginning work on the history of a very different progressive school, the Downtown Community School in New York City, a school founded more in the social reconstructionist model than the individual child centered model of Dalton. This school, unlike Dalton, did not survive. As historians of education write the histories of progressive schools, we will be in a better position to answer historical and policy questions. Thus, while this historical case study of the Dalton School has limited generalizability beyond the walls of the school, I hope it becomes data for ongoing comparative-historical analysis.

Finally, I hope historical research on progressive education provides current educators with some necessary historical perspective. At a time when educators believe they have invented new methods, such as whole language, integrated curriculum, and cooperative learning, they would do well to remember that progressives in the 1920s and 1930s used similar approaches under the names of core curriculum and project method. Rather than constantly reinventing the wheel, educators could learn a great deal from the study of the history of education. If there is a policy concern of this book, I guess this is it. Perhaps through the profiles in the Chapter 8 of teachers such as Tessie Ross educators will remember that good education leads to what philosopher Maxine Greene calls "wide awakeness." That Dalton provided a place for teachers like Tessie to teach children and to mentor teachers (including me) is an important part of its legacy. That it no longer is the school in which Tessie taught is a central argument of this book. Why this is the case is the purpose of historical research and hopefully I have provided some answers.

In the last analysis, what the school is uniquely equipped to do, given the range of agencies that educate, is to make youngsters aware of the constant bombardment of facts, opinions, and values to which they are subjected; to help them question what they see and hear; and, ultimately, to give them the intellectual resources they need to make judgements and assess significance.

Lawrence A. Cremin,
The Genius of American Education

1

INTRODUCTION

The Dalton School is a coeducational, independent day school located on the fashionable Upper East Side of Manhattan. At present, the Middle and High School, grades four through twelve are housed in a ten story brick building at 108 East 89th Street. The Lower School, grades K through three are housed in two cleverly connected townhouses at 53 and 61 East 91st Street.

The neighborhood in which the school is located contains some of the most costly real estate in this country. Apartment prices generally range from half of a million dollars to over several million dollars. It is a neighborhood of extreme wealth, loosely bounded on the north by 96th Street; on the south by 59th Street; encompassing Third through Fifth Avenues. Politicians refer to it as the "Silk Stocking" district of New York; its residents tend to vote Republican.

It is readily apparent to those who approach the school from Park Avenue, an avenue of trees with islands of cultivated greenery in the middle, that the neighborhood is one of elegance and affluence. Regal apartment houses of neo-classical or Beaux Arts design, constructed in the 1920s and 1930s line both sides of the avenue. A sense of wealth and well-being is further underscored by the early morning scene of white gloved, uniformed doormen hailing taxis or opening doors of limousines for smartly attired, mostly white building residents on their way to Wall Street law or investment banking firms, or somewhat later, their clubs or shopping excursions downtown.

At 8:00 A.M. and 3:30 P.M. the serenity of the neighborhood is abruptly shattered by seemingly endless waves of students boisterously winding their way down 89th Street, jostling each other with their backpacks as they surge through the front and side doors of the school and line up by the elevators to the right of the doors. Some of these students have traveled by subway to reach the school either from Greenwich Village, Brooklyn, or the Bronx. The majority, however, have "bused it" or "cabbed it," from either the West Side or the East Side, the latter usually well within walking distance of the school. Still others, frequently the latecomers, are the lucky ones who have only to "fall out of bed," hastily dress and bound up the block to school.

Apart from these tidal waves of students at set times of the day, unwary visitors may fail to recognize the true identity of the building which houses the school. Unlike the typical institutional style architecture of many urban and suburban schools, the 89th Street building was purposely constructed to blend in with the neighborhood. Thus, it could easily be mistaken for an apartment house, save for its protective black wrought iron gates ringing its graceful brick facade. Only a careful observation will reveal the sign, "the Dalton School," placed discreetly above the lintel of the main entranceway (and which was so indiscreetly displayed by filmmaker Woody Allen in his cinematic work, *Manhattan*).

The frankly dignified exterior of the building, especially during the winter, belies the scene of pandemonium which often greets visitors to the school as they enter through the lobby. Because Dalton is an urban school, and the 89th Street building houses over twice the amount of students it was built to house, space is at a premium. To the consternation of the administration, high school students have staked out the lobby of the school as their territory. Thus, for most of the school day the ground floor is inhabited by high school students "hanging out"; their population density is determined by individual schedules and by the weather. Visitors to the school must gingerly pick their way through piles of bookbags, backpacks or reclining bodies of adolescents to reach the elevators.

Recently, to alleviate the congestion in the lobby and perhaps to lessen the visual effect of the lounging adolescents frequently draped over each other, the administration has built a contained arrangement of semi-circular benches on a raised platform directly beyond the front entrance. This cleverly designed seating configuration both entices students to gather in the contained area while its raised sides shields the students from full view of visitors to the school. The results have only been partially successful since seating capacity is limited.

If the lobby is the domain of the High School, the street directly in front of the school belongs to the Middle School every Monday through Friday at lunch hour. It is at these times that the school legally bars traffic from 89th Street, while Middle School students engage in the urban phenomenon known as "Play Street"; then, children's games, most often played in school yards, are played by Dalton students in the street (probably the only street play experience most of these students will have), while neighborhood inhabitants carefully negotiate their paths along the sidewalks dodging stray balls, frisbees and energetic children.

Changes in the weather abruptly alter the landscape surrounding the 89th Street building. As the weather becomes warmer, in spring and in fall, a casual visitor to the area would most certainly be aware of the presence of a school. Sidewalk traffic increases, but this traffic is comprised of adolescents, often attired in clothing associated with camping, or other outdoor leisure activities, lounging or sunbathing in the doorways of neighboring apartment houses or brownstones. Indeed, to the bane of the school's immediate neighbors, the block often takes on a beach-like atmosphere as students, clad in shorts and tee shirts, take to the streets with walk-men in tow, eager to socialize with friends, smoke forbidden cigarettes or catch a few "rays."

Two blocks up from the 89th Street building a more subdued atmosphere prevails throughout the year at the 91st Street facility, which houses the Lower School, also referred to as the First Program. Located on a quiet tree lined street of townhouses, few children are visible to visitors to the area, save at arrival and dismissal times. Then, pandemonium prevails here too, as private buses, limousines, taxis and assorted luxury cars, usually of foreign origin, block traffic on the street, disgorging or collecting their charges.

While the majority of students at the 89th Street building travel to school by themselves, those at 91st Street must be transported by car or escorted, either by parents, nannies, housekeepers or au pairs. This in part accounts for the fact that most of the students in the First Program are fairly affluent and white, and live within the confines of the neighborhood. The other factor which determines racial composition at 91st Street is the tuition. Parents of Dalton students pay an average tuition of $12,000 per year to send their children to school. They are also solicited for voluntary contributions of several hundred dollars above the tuition, school benefits and the endowment fund. Thus, sending a child to Dalton (or any comparable independent school in the area) is an expensive proposition; in fact, the current headmaster, Gardner Dunnan, has frequently noted that parents who have incomes totaling $100,000.00 are just "making it." Scholarship monies are available and currently 18% of the student body receives scholarship aid; however, a disproportionate amount, 21% is concentrated in the High School. This would account for the more socially and economically mixed student body in the Upper School; lesser ones in the Middle School and First Program.

Because of the costliness of sending children to Dalton, the school must struggle to maintain a diverse student body. Under its founder Helen Parkhurst and her successor, Charlotte Durham, the school was a haven for the children of professionals in the arts, intellectuals, affluent, successful German Jews and WASPs interested in progressive education. There was always a commitment to minority representation and to financial aid. This configuration shifted somewhat under Donald Barr, as the student body almost tripled in size and the physical plant expanded to 91st and 94th Streets (where a gymnasium is housed). Increasingly, the children of German Jews and WASPs were eclipsed by a large cohort of children of newly affluent, successful, often high profile, predominately Eastern European Jews.[1] This trend has continued under Gardner Dunnan, although recently there has been a serious effort to attract more minority students to Dalton. Nevertheless, the student body that visitors encounter today reflects a significant number of children of affluent, successful, talented and visible individuals in real estate, investment banking, law, medicine and the fashion industry. Children of intellectuals and children of parents in the arts are also represented; today the difference being that these children are often the

---

[1]The tensions between German Jews, who first arrived in the United States in the mid-19th century and Eastern European Jews, who arrived later in the late 19th and early 20th century, has been well documented. This conflict was economic, cultural, and religious. It involved issues of assimilation and status competition, as well as conflicts originating in Europe. In the early 20th century, German Jews who had already assimilated into the upper middle class, often resented the working class culture of the new immigrant Eastern European Jews. As Eastern European Jews assimilated as well in the coming decades, they were often seen by affluent German Jews as examples of "new money." For a discussion of these conflicts see, Richard L. Zweigenhaft and G. William Domhoff, *Jews in the Protestant Establishment* (New York: Praeger, 1982) and *Blacks in the White Establishment?* (New Haven: Yale University Press, 1991), pp. 168–170. What is important is that as the school's population increasingly included assimilated Eastern European Jews, the conflict between this economically and culturally ascending group and German Jews, who made up a significant portion of the Dalton community in the early years, is an important part of the school's history.

offspring of more affluent, more established and less media shy individuals than in past decades. It is this trend from a low profile, frequently offbeat parent body, to a successful, high profile one, which has created both negative and positive images of the school.

Returning to the First Program, little of the high profile image of the school is present as visitors pause at 51 East 91st Street. Rather, visitors to the school are struck by an aura of order and tradition, suggested by the location as well as the architectural facade of the building. Few parents applying to the First Program at Dalton today are actually aware or interested in Dalton's progressive roots. Significantly at one open house, prospective parents posed many questions, however, "None of them were about the school's philosophy or operation. All were related directly or indirectly to the admissions process. "What do you have to do to get in?" one father asked."[2] Perhaps this incident is an important indication not only of the lack of knowledge of the progressive tradition Dalton represents, but also the current concerns of parents when admission to the school is the bottom line—a group buying a credential rather than a particular educational philosophy. In any event, the setting of the school at 91st Street would scarcely indicate Dalton's roots in an important historical movement in education, which has dominated educational thinking for so much of this century: progressive education.

* * *

Progressive education has dominated educational thinking for much of the century, so much so that "by the mid-1940s it was no longer referred to as progressive education but as "modern education" or the "new educational practice."[3] Nevertheless, it is an all but impossible task to provide a "capsule definition of progressive education."[4] This is due to its numerous

---

[2]Bernice Kanner, "The Admissions Go-Round: Private School Fever," *New York Magazine*, November 23, 1987, p. 45.

[3]Diane Ravitch, *The Troubled Crusade* (New York: Basic Books, 1983), p. 43.

[4]Lawrence A. Cremin, *The Transformation of the School* (New York: Alfred A. Knopf, 1961) p. X.

and contradictory strands.[5] It is safe to say, however, that progressive education began as a movement roughly about the same time as Progressivism began as the political reform movement and must be understood against this larger backdrop:

> Actually, progressive education began as part of a vast humanitarian effort to apply the promise of American life. The ideal of government by, of, and for the people—to the puzzling new urban-industrial civilization that came into being during the latter half of the nineteenth century. The word *progressive* provides the clue to what it really was: the educational phase of American progressive education *writ large.*[6]

Accordingly, in order to fully understand the movement in which the Dalton School was born, it is necessary to examine the larger historical movement of which progressive education was a part; then proceed to look, if briefly, at an important American philosopher who helped shape the thinking of progressive educators: John Dewey.

The beginning of the nineteenth century ushered in the First Industrial Revolution, immigration and urbanization of unprecedented proportions. The conditions created by these events were met with responses from social reformers whose concerns were far reaching and who attempted to address and redress the evils of American life. Yet, if the beginning of

---

[5]For a more detailed discussion of the history of progressive education see Lawrence A. Cremin, *The Transformation of the School* (New York: Alfred A. Knopf, 1961); Lawrence A. Cremin, *American Education: The Metropolitan Experience* (New York: Harper and Row, 1988); Merle Curti, *The Social Ideas of American Educators* (New York: Charles Scribner and Sons, 1935); Patricia Albjerg Graham, *Progressive Education: From Arcady to Academe* (New York: Teachers College Press, 1967); Diane Ravitch, *The Troubled Crusade* (New York: Basic Books, 1983); Harold Rugg and Ann Shumaker, *The Child Centered School* (New York: Arno Press, 1969); David B. Tyack, *The One Best System* (Cambridge: Harvard University Press, 1974).

[6]Lawrence A. Cremin, *The Transformation of the School*, p. viii.

the nineteenth century seemed problematic to Americans, the close of the century must have been even more so. Again, there was a revolution in industry, referred to as the Second Industrial Revolution, but this time it involved steam driven and electric powered machinery. Factories had given way to gigantic corporations, under the control of such captains of industry, as Andrew Carnegie, John D. Rockefeller and Cornelius Vanderbilt. Significantly, immigrant labor played an essential role in this revolution.

At the beginning of the nineteenth century, the largest number of immigrants to the United States came from the northwestern part of Europe, namely Great Britain, Scandinavia, Germany, and the Netherlands. After 1890, an increasingly larger number of immigrants came from southern and eastern Europe. These immigrants' languages, customs, and living styles were dramatically different from the previous group. They settled in closely crowded substandard living quarters in urban areas, and found work in factories. Thus American cities, by the turn of the century, contained both enormous concentrations of wealth and enormous concentrations of poverty. Indeed, the gap between rich and poor had never been as great as it was at the close of the nineteenth century.

It was at this juncture, the period between 1900-1914, that a new reform movement of unprecedented proportions would sweep the country: the Progressive Movement. Progressive reformers insisted upon government regulation of industry and commerce, government regulation and conservation of the nation's natural resources; moreover, progressive reformers insisted that government at national, state, and local levels be responsive to the welfare of its citizens rather than to the welfare of corporations. Significantly, progressive reformers had a sweeping agenda, ranging from a secret ballot to schooling. As social reformers, such as Horace Mann in the nineteenth century, looked to schools as means of addressing social problems, this time social reformers, such as John Dewey, once again looked to schools; this time as a means of preserving and promoting democracy, within the new social order.

John Dewey (1859-1952) was an important philosopher of American pragmatism. A contemporary of such reformers as "Fighting Bob La Follette," governor of Wisconsin and architect of the "Wisconsin Idea," which harnessed the expertise of university professors to the mechanics of state government; settlement workers, such as Jane Addams and Lillian Wald; municipal reformers and labor leaders, such as Henry Bruere and John Golden, Dewey sought to link philosophy to human problems.

Although Dewey was born and raised in rural Vermont, by 1894, he had become thoroughly immeshed in the problems of urbanization as a resident of Chicago and Chair of the Department of Philosophy, Psychology, and Pedagogy at the University of Chicago. Distressed with the abrupt dislocation of families from rural to urban environments; concerned with the loss of traditional ways of understanding the maintenance of civilization; anxious about the effects unleashed individualism and rampant materialism would have upon a democratic society, Dewey sought answers in pedagogic practice.

Dewey argued particularly, in *My Pedagogic Creed*, *The School and Society* and *The Child and the Curriculum* for a restructuring of schools along the lines of "embryonic communities" and for the creation of a curriculum which would allow for the child's interests and developmental level, while introducing the child to, "the point of departure from which the child can trace and follow the progress of mankind in history, getting an insight also into the materials used and the mechanical principles involved."[7]

Dewey believed that the end of education was growth, which was firmly posited within a democratic society. Thus, school, for Dewey was "that form of community life in which all those agencies are concentrated that will be most effective in bringing the child to share in the inherited resources of the race, and to use his own powers for social ends."[8]

To implement his ideas, Dewey created the Laboratory School at the University of Chicago. There, children studied basic subjects in an integrated curriculum, since according to Dewey, "the child's life is an integral, a total one and therefore, the school should reflect the "completeness" and "unity" of the "child's own world."[9] Dewey advocated active learning, starting with the needs and interests of the child; he emphasized the role of experience in education and introduced the notion of teacher as facilitator of learning, rather than the font from which all knowledge flows. The school, according to Dewey, was a "miniature community and

---

[7]Martin S. Dworkin, ed. *Dewey on Education* (New York: Teachers College Press, 1959), p. 43.

[8]Ibid., p.22.

[9]Ibid., p. 93.

embryonic society,"[10] and discipline was a tool which would develop "a spirit of social cooperation and community life." [11]

That John Dewey made important contributions to both philosophy of education and pedagogic practice is undisputable. What is particularly important here is his influence upon a group of practitioners who under his influence, founded independent progressive schools throughout the country which mirrored his Laboratory School, a school which, "tried to provide education that balanced the children's interests with the knowledge of adults, that engaged the children in cooperative, active work, and that integrated social and intellectual learning...(a school in which) the concepts of growth and active learning imbued the curriculum."[12]

While progressive education may be impossible to define, other than to conclude, as does Diane Ravitch, that "it was an attitude, a belief in experimentation, a commitment to the education of all children and to democracy in the schools,"[13] nevertheless there are, as Lawrence A. Cremin suggests, four dominant themes present throughout the movement:

1. a broadening of the school to include a direct concern for health, vocation, and the quality of community life;

2. the application in the classroom of more humane, more active, and more rational pedagogical techniques derived from research in philosophy, psychology, and the social sciences;

3. the tailoring of instruction more directly to the different kinds and classes of children who were being brought within the purview of school...;

4. and finally, the use of more systematic and rational

---

[10]Ibid., p. 41.

[11]Ibid., p. 40.

[12]Carl F. Kaestle, "The Public Schools and The Public Mood," *American Heritage*, February, 1990, p. 74.

[13]Diane Ravitch, p. 44.

approaches to the administration and management of the schools.[14]

*   *   *

Before the 1920s progressive reformers tended to concentrate their efforts in public education, applying scientific management techniques to the administration of schools,[15] reforming curriculum and creating secondary, vocational schools. As Cremin suggests, during the 1920s many progressive educators began to focus "on a select group of pedagogical innovative independent schools catering principally to middle class children."[16] Such a school was the Dalton School, founded by Helen Parkhurst, coincidentally as World War I was drawing to a close and "a great divide in the history of progressive education"[17] was occurring—one in which the thrust toward "social reformism was virtually eclipsed by the rhetoric of child-centered pedagogy."[18]

Dalton was also founded at a time when "progressive private day schools began to emerge in growing numbers."[19] These schools, often the creation of parent cooperatives or talented practitioners held the common practice that, "each individual has uniquely creative potentialities and that a school in which children are encouraged freely to develop their potential is the best guarantee of a larger society truly devoted to human worth and

---

[14]Lawrence A. Cremin, *American Education: The Metropolitan Experience* (New York: Harper and Row, 1988), p. 229. I have quoted Cremin's exact words, however, I have taken the liberty of separating and numbering each theme he discusses.

[15]For a detailed discussion of administrative progressives see David B. Tyack and Elisabeth Hansot, *Managers of Virtue: Public School Leadership in America, 1920-1980* (New York: Basic Books, 1982).

[16]Lawrence A. Cremin, *The Metropolitan Experience*, p. 229.

[17]Lawrence A. Cremin, *The Transformation of the School*, p. 179.

[18]Ibid., p. 181.

[19]Otto F. Kraushaar, *American Nonpublic Schools: Patterns of Diversity* (Baltimore and London: Johns Hopkins University Press, 1972) p. 81.

excellence."[20]

These schools, commonly referred to by educators as "child-centered" were often founded by female practitioners "spurred by the revolt against "the harsh pedagogy" of the existing schools and by the ferment of change and new thought of the first two decades of the twentieth century."[21] While many historians tend to group these schools together, nevertheless, each has a distinct philosophy and practice according to the particular vision of its founder. For example, City and Country, founded by Caroline Pratt emphasized the notion of self-expression and growth through play; in particular through play with wooden blocks.[22] Another school, such as The Walden School, founded by Margaret Naumburg who was heavily influenced by Freudian psychology, emphasized the notion of "individual transformation." Under the leadership of Naumburg's sister, Florence Cane, the school encouraged "children to paint exactly what they felt impelled to paint."[23] Other examples include The Bank Street School, founded by Lucy Sprague Mitchell,[24] and The Lincoln School, founded by Abraham Flexner, which became a laboratory school for Teachers College, Columbia University.[25] Outside of New York City, where each of these schools were founded, were other examples of progressive education. Among these were the The Putney School, a boarding school in Putney, Vermont, founded by Carmelita Hinton,[26] Francis W. Parker

---

[20]Lawrence A. Cremin, *The Transformation of the School*, p. 202.

[21]Otto F. Kraushaar, p. 81.

[22]For a full discussion of Caroline Pratt's philosophy see her book, *Experimental Practice in the City and Country School* (New York: E.P. Dutton and Co., 1924).

[23]Lawrence A. Cremin, *The Transformation of the School*, p. 213.

[24]See Joyce Antler, *Lucy Sprague Mitchell: The Making of a Modern Woman* (New Haven: Yale University Press, 1987).

[25]For a discussion of the relationship between Teachers College and the Lincoln School and a detailed description of its progressive pedagogic practices see Lawrence A. Cremin, *The Transformation of the School*, pp. 280–286.

[26]See Amanda Katie Geer, *The Putney School, Examined Through the Life of Carmelita Chase Hinton* (Putney, VT: The Putney School, 1982) and Susan Lloyd, *The Putney School: A Progressive Experiment* (New Haven:

School in Chicago, founded by one of the early pioneers of progressive pedagogy, Colonel Francis W. Parker,[27] and The Shady Hill School in Cambridge, Massachusetts.[28]

The Dalton School, founded by Helen Parkhurst, while falling under the rubric of a child-centered school, nevertheless differs significantly from both City and Country, Walden, and the others. As this book will demonstrate, Parkhurst's particular philosophy, education on the Dalton Plan, was an interesting and innovative synthesis of the ideas of John Dewey and more particularly, Carleton W. Washburne, the latter, architect of education on the individual system introduced in the public schools of Winnetka, Illinois.[29]

It was Parkhurst's mission and also her genius to interest people in her ideas about education on the Dalton Plan, and to solicit financial support from them as well; at first, to establish the school; then, to ensure its maintenance. In both areas she was enormously successful. Her book, *Education On the Dalton Plan*, was translated into many languages, including Spanish, Italian, Japanese, Russian and Dutch. Dalton Schools were established in the United Kingdom, Japan, The Netherlands, Russia,

---

Yale University Press, 1987).

[27]See Marie Stone, ed. *Between Home and Community: Chronicle of the Francis W. Parker School* (Chicago: Francis W. Parker School, 1976). For Parker's writings on progressive pedagogy see Francis W. Parker, *Talks on Pedagogics* (New York: A.S. Barnes and Co., 1894) and *Talks on Teaching* (New York: E.L. Kellogg and Co., 1903).

[28]See Edward Yeomans, *The Shady Hill School: The First Fifty Years* (Cambridge: Windflower Press, 1979).

[29]For a more complete discussion of the work of Carleton W. Washburne, see Lawrence A. Cremin, *The Transformation of the School*, pp. 295–299. See also Washburne's own writings, including, Carleton W. Washburne, *Adjusting the School to the Child* (New York: World Book Company, 1932) and Carleton W. Washburne and Sidney P. Maryland, Jr. *Winnetka: The History and Significance of an Educational Experiment* (Engelwood Cliffs, N.J.: Prentice Hall, 1963).

and Chile.[30] The Dalton School in New York still stands, a living testimony to her vision and perseverance. Helen Parkhurst remained headmistress of the school she founded from 1919 to 1942,[31] after which she was succeeded by Charlotte Durham, former chairman of the High School.

As founder of the Dalton School and promoter of the Dalton Plan, Helen Parkhurst was in an enviable position: she could do no wrong.[32] Her constituents—trustees, most of whom had children in the school, many of whom were on scholarship; parents, faculty, and students excited by the experimentalism inherent in the nature of the institution—trusted her to make educational and financial decisions. Her behavior, often eccentric, often tyrannical, was tolerated for she was "Parkie." Thus, Helen Parkhurst "ran" Dalton for over twenty years until crushing financial problems galvanized the Board of Trustees into demanding her resignation.

The history of Helen Parkhurst's administration and the subsequent administrations of Charlotte Durham, Jack Kittell, Donald Barr, and Gardner Dunnan[33] illustrate an important theme in the history of Dalton, namely, that the head of the school makes the school what it is; that "life in a school—the quality of its culture—... (is) in large part a function of its principal."[34] Roland Barth, in *Run School Run*, states that, "Only recently

---

[30]In the United Kingdom, a number of books on the Dalton Plan were published, including C.W. Kimmins and Belle Rennie, *The Triumph of the Dalton Plan* (London: Nicholson and Watson, Ltd., 1923), for which Helen Parkhurst wrote a foreword. A. J. Lynch, *The Rise and Progress of the Dalton Plan* (London: George Philip and Son, 1926) and *Individual Work and the Dalton Plan* (London: George Philip and Son, 1924).

[31]There are many discrepancies over the exact date as to when the Dalton School was founded. After sifting through numerous documents and talking to people, many of whom have failing memories, I have chosen 1919 as the most probable date.

[32]Professor David Rothman in a speech delivered to the Dalton Faculty during the academic year of 1980–81.

[33]Although I will discuss the Kittell years, which were brief, my analysis of leadership throughout the book includes only the four major school heads: Parkhurst, Durham, Barr, and Dunnan.

[34]Seymour B. Sarason, *The Culture of the School and the Problem of Change* (Boston: Allyn and Bacon, 1971), p. 207.

have educational policy makers come to realize, for instance, that the school principal has an extraordinary influence over the quality of education and the quality of life under the roof of the schoolhouse."[35] And Otto F. Kraushaar, in writing about America's nonpublic schools, suggests that,

> The success or failure of private schools depends to a large extent upon the quality of the school head's leadership. Whereas the public school principal characteristically is subject to the control of a central administration and guided by detailed, carefully spelled out procedures, the private school head works within an autonomous domain. In principle at least, the private school is directed from within and is responsible only to its board, its clients and supporters, not to government bureaus or to the public at large. And since most governing boards of private schools customarily delegate broad powers to the head—powers that reside legally in the trustees—it is the quality of the head or succession of heads that makes or breaks a school.[36]

There are of course, many other significant factors that contribute to an independent day school's success or failure. One in particular, in Dalton's case was neighborhood. The Dalton School began in a brownstone on the Upper West Side. In the same year that the stock market collapsed, 1929, the school fortuitously moved to the Upper East Side, its present location on East 89th Street. Although at the time of its move there was grave concern about financing the building; nevertheless, in moving, the school was ultimately spared the subsequent demographic upheaval which occurred in its former location. It was also able to draw a steady applicant

---

[35]Roland Barth, *Run School Run* (Cambridge, Mass., and London: Harvard University Press, 1980), p. xvi. For further discussion of the importance of school heads see Gerald Grant, *The World We Created at Hamilton High* (Cambridge: Harvard Press, 1988), Ch. 8; also Sara Lawrence Lightfoot, *The Good High School* (New York: Basic Books, 1984).

[36]Kraushaar, p. 173–174.

pool from its immediate new neighborhood, a group fully able to pay the continuously rising tuition rates.

A second important factor, external to the head of the school is the spirit of the times or the *Zeitgeist*. In a liberal climate, many parents will consciously seek out experimental schools for their children; then, as conservatism sets in, they will revert to more traditionally oriented schools. Indeed, the success or failure of particular schools may be measured in part, against the cycles of American educational reform, which historian Diane Ravitch illuminates in her book, *The Troubled Crusade*.

A third factor, wholly inexplicable by any rational means is the phenomenon of the "hot" school. Certain schools seemingly overnight, become desirable, especially to a particular group of New York cognoscenti whose reading tends to be more oriented to such publications as publisher John Fairchild's "W" than *The New York Review of Books*.

However, Otto Kraushaar's notion that the broad decision-making powers reside with the head of the school, that it is the head of the school who sets the tone and direction of the school and is responsible for its success or failure, is, as I will argue in the following pages, crucial to the history of Dalton. It is true that constituent bodies exist: trustees, teachers, parents, students. However, each group is tied to the head in some telling way and each changes, dramatically in some cases, within a relatively brief period its composition.

For example, let us look at Dalton's Board of Trustees. In 1955–56, there were twenty-six board members. Of the twenty-six, one member represented the faculty; the remainder were parents, and within this group, two represented alumni; a third, the parent-teacher association. Trustees at Dalton usually have children in the school; these children are ultimately college bound. Additionally, trustees' terms are fixed and most work; thus they can only be depended upon to devote a small percentage of their time to the institution since most have demanding businesses or professions to maintain. In terms of continuity, during 1968–69, there were only three people listed as board members who had served in 1955–56. And of these three, two, Mrs. William Rosenwald and Mrs. W. Murray Crane, were listed as honorary trustees.

As for the faculty, while there was an impressive degree of continuity between those who worked for Helen Parkhurst and those who worked for Charlotte Durham, there was a large exodus of Charlotte Durham's staff shortly after Donald Barr's appointment. Another occurred after Gardner Dunnan's as well. Faculty members at Dalton are untenured. Many move, change occupations, and retire. Still, there are a few remaining members on the staff today, such as Aaron Kurzen, Harold Aks, Margot Gumport, and Alan Boyers, who worked for Charlotte Durham. The parent body as well reflects the trend of the faculty. Continuity exists through alumni children, now students at Dalton; however, there is probably more "new blood" than old Dalton families enrolled in the school at present.

Ultimately, the decision-making powers remain with the head of the school. It is he or she who decides to what extent and how the philosophy is to be implemented, which faculty members will receive contracts, who is to be admitted. From time to time, as financial problems arise, the head becomes vulnerable to criticism and may, indeed, be pressed to resign. But when the budget is balanced, the word of the head of the school is law: "...power does not reside in an individual, anymore than authority rests in a position. Power is a property of a social relationship; it is an individual's capacity to influence someone or some group."[37] It is also important to note that each head of Dalton has had a group of individuals, either informal or formal, not unlike a regime in the historical sense of the word. Each regime provided the head with information to facilitate decision-making; each regime disseminated information to the school at large. Although it cannot be documented, certain individuals within particular regimes probably had some important decision-making powers. And one particular head had the capacity to influence a new group that came to dominate the parent body of the school.

Just "who" composed particular regimes is difficult to say since I have found in my work that memories are short, animosities are long, and in both instances, rumors abound. I can, nevertheless, state with some certainty that Parkhurst had the support of particular trustees, parents, and teachers who believed her to be the messiah of progressive education. And, of course, there were powerful trustees and parents alike who were grateful that Dalton accepted and educated their children—children who would have had difficulty functioning in such traditional schools as Collegiate or Brearley.

Several informants regarding Charlotte Durham's administration

---

[37]Francis A.J. Ianni and Elizabeth Reuss Ianni, *A Family Business* (Hartford: Russell Sage Foundation, 1972), p. 115.

point to a group of "WASP lawyers" who supposedly acted as her loyal supporters and advisors; others, to Stanley Isaacs, her Treasurer, as her primary advisor for it was Isaacs, as we shall see, who rescued the school from bankruptcy and balanced the budget. Durham worked with parent and teacher groups as well, consulting with them regularly. She asked for input from a variety of individuals and organizations, such as the PTA and the Associates (a select group of parents of Dalton students); she established an administration marked by constant dialogue between the headmistress and the various constituents of the school.

Jack Kittell did not succeed in influencing the Dalton community; in his brief tenure as headmaster he failed to secure a group of individuals who would support his policies. This was not the case, however, with Donald Barr.

The Barr "regime" contained a loyal group of trustees, administrators, faculty, parents and students who acted as informants, disseminators of information and who made many decisions attributed to Barr. Informants vary as to who actually constituted Barr's "inner circle"; for our purpose it is important to note that his supporters believed in Barr's educational philosophy and supported Barr's hard line disciplinary actions regarding drugs, political demonstrations, and dress regulations.

These individuals seemed to come from a new ethnic group at Dalton; a group which would provide Barr with the authority and power the Iannis discuss in their book, *A Family Business*. This new group to which I allude was the previously discussed parent group composed primarily of Jews of Eastern European origin along with a smattering of Columbia University intelligentsia (the latter referred to as "Barr's Mafia"). This group had access to the media, it was composed of many powerful people, upwardly mobile and newly monied. This "new group" supported Donald Barr's hard-line approach to drugs and his emphasis upon academic rigor. It felt comfortable with Donald Barr's "homey" personal style, his crewcut and his red suspenders.

It was this group of "New Daltonians" that gave Donald Barr the mandate he needed to implement radical change in the school. More significantly, it was this group that saved him his position as headmaster in 1970, when leaders of the "Old Dalton" group, consisting of members of prominent old New York German Jewish families and a smattering of gentiles, espousing more liberal views than Barr's, sought to force his resignation. It is important to keep his demographic shift in mind when reading about "The Barr Years."

The demographic shift begun during the Barr administration continues through the Dunnan administration. Thus, the parent and student bodies today differ even more so than those in the early years. Trustees as well reflect the change, as most of the Board members are currently Dalton parents. Additionally, there are fewer and fewer "Old Bolsheviks" among the faculty. As the past becomes more distant, memories grow dim. Indeed, some of the newer teachers think the philosophy of the school, the Dalton Plan, is an insurance benefit package. Again, the head is the constant in the configuration of trustees, parents, students, faculty for all ultimately depend upon the head in some way. Where Dunnan's regime differs from previous administrators is in his construction of a hierarchial bureaucracy that governs the school on a daily basis.

This history of Dalton is a history that focuses on leadership and the way leadership reflects, rejects, or compromises contemporary reform movements and current cultural concerns. It is also, in sum, the history of the transformation of a school from a small, independent, experimental, progressive school to a large, academically rigorous, independent institution with a progressive tradition, namely the Dalton Plan.

2

HELEN PARKHURST:
THE FOUNDER AND THE PLAN

The Dalton School, in its early years, perdured because of Helen Parkhurst. Her vision and force of personality engendered great loyalty from her faculty, school parents, board of trustees, and students. Her particular form of progressive education, which came to be known as the Dalton Plan, was adopted in places as distant as Japan. But Helen Parkhurst, the woman, was an anomaly. Her competence as an educator was unquestionable, but on the personal level she exhibited a single-minded persuasiveness, a driving ambition, and an unparalleled ability to use people to achieve her own ends. I believe that her entrepreneurial approach to education, acceptable in the 1920s, her forceful personality, and her single-minded determination were responsible for The Dalton Plan taking root in the Children's University School, renamed the Dalton School in 1920.

The history of the Dalton School and the life of its founder, Helen Parkhurst, are intertwined from the years between 1916 and 1942. It is important to examine Parkhurst's early years if we are to discover how her educational philosophy was formed. According to her *curriculum vitae*,[1] she was born in Durand, Wisconsin, in 1887. She excelled in high school, graduating as her class valedictorian. In college, at Wisconsin State, she completed four years in two, graduating in 1907 with the highest professional honors ever awarded.

Although no direct documentation exists, it is probable that Helen Parkhurst came under the influence of Frederic Burk and Carleton Washburne, the latter having developed the "individual system,"[2] which allowed students to progress through their studies at their own pace. Parkhurst, however, dubbed the philosophical underpinnings of her approach the Dalton Laboratory Plan, and emphasized the laboratory, or "lab," as her

---

[1] See Helen Parkhurst, "Curriculum Vitae" (New York: Dalton School Archives, n.d.), n.p. (mimeographed).

[2] Lawrence A. Cremin, *The Transformation of the School* (New York: Alfred A. Knopf, 1961), pp. 295–96.

students and faculty came to call it, as her own unique creation, and one of the focal concepts of her plan. She claimed to have discovered lab as a teacher in a normal school at age sixteen. Small, frail, and not knowing much mathematics, Helen Parkhurst had to cope with teaching this subject to a group of farm boys, some of whom were far larger and knew more than she. Parkhurst grouped the students around a table in the rear of the classroom and in an early instance of peer instruction, had the older, more knowledgeable students help and instruct the younger.[3] Thus, the laboratory was born out of pressing need and ingenuity.

In 1914, while on leave as Director of the Primary Training Department of Central State College in Stevens Point, Wisconsin, Helen Parkhurst was appointed by the Wisconsin State Department of Education to report on the Montessori Method. Parkhurst studied in Rome with Maria Montessori, and, according to her, became the only person ever authorized by Montessori herself to train teachers.[4]

According to Helen Parkhurst, she never returned to Stevens Point, Wisconsin, but rather went directly to found the Dalton School. To the contrary, historical evidence, points to the fact that Parkhurst did return to Stevens Point, where she taught until 1915.[5] It is probably around 1915--1916 that her rather fortuitous relationship with Mrs. W. Murray Crane began, the woman who was to provide Helen Parkhurst with the financial support she needed to found her school. Mrs. W. Murray Crane, a mid-Westerner by birth, transplanted by marriage to a pastoral factory town in Dalton, Massachusetts, was the second wife of one of the wealthiest men in America. The Crane family business, founded in 1801, is printing paper: paper for stationery and paper for the United States Mint. The Cranes had three children: two boys and one girl, Louise, the youngest, born in 1913.

---

[3]Helen Parkhurst relayed the incident to former Dalton teacher Nora Hodges in 1936. Interview with Mrs. Nora Hodges, January 24, 1979. There is some discrepancy between Parkhurst's account of her physical vulnerability and of those who knew her as a tall, imposing woman. Perhaps at age sixteen, she had not fully matured physically.

[4]Marilyn Feldman, "Helen Parkhurst: (New York: Dalton School Archives, 1977), p. 3 (mimeographed).

[5]Former UW-SP teacher honored at dedication," *Stevens Point (Wisc.) Daily Journal*, March 4, 1974.

It was the education of Louise Crane that Helen Parkhurst was invited to Dalton, Massachusetts, to supervise. There is little documentation regarding just how and precisely when Helen Parkhurst began her school for Louise Crane and three or four of her friends in the Crane family house in Dalton, Massachusetts. What is of particular significance here is the relationship began by the two women: one rich, powerful and an important patron of the arts; the other, a practitioner of modest means, and a messiah of progressive education.

Parkhurst's school in Mrs. W. Murray Crane's house lasted according to Winthrop Crane, for one year[6]; she then went on to implement the Dalton Plan in the public high school in Dalton, Massachusetts. This too, lasted for one year. Although difficult to document, it has been suggested that the relative brevity of the experiment was due to parental resistance, perhaps portending the fate of similar experiments in public high schools in New York City. It was after this abortive experiment in the public sector that with the encouragement and financial support from Mrs. W. Murray Crane, Helen Parkhurst opened the Dalton School in New York City in 1919. Her school, originally called The Children's University School, was renamed the Dalton School in 1920; a compromise perhaps, since Helen Parkhurst, according to informants, wanted to name the school after her benefactor who declined the honor (and perhaps the publicity) in favor of the name of the town from which the Crane family originated. Her particular progressive pedagogical plan, originally called the Laboratory Plan, was also renamed the Dalton Plan in keeping with the new name of the school.

The original site of Helen Parkhurst's school was a brownstone on West 74th Street. As the school began to increase its student body, larger quarters became necessary. Thus, the Lower School was moved to West 72nd Street and the High School was opened on West 73rd Street. In the Fall of 1929, both divisions were moved to one of the school's present

---

[6]Interview with Mr. Winthrop Crane, August 8, 1991. There is some discrepancy about when Parkhurt's Plan was adopted in the high school in Dalton, MA. I have chosen Winthrop Crane's account, although Carleton Washburne dates it at 1920.

locations at 108 East 89th Street.[7]

Helen Parkhurst's early educational efforts attracted a great deal of attention. It was said that John Dewey was a frequent visitor to Dalton;[8] Evelyn Dewey published *The Dalton Laboratory Plan* in 1922, devoting an entire chapter to the Children's University School in operation. But Parkhurst, herself, was her own best publicist. Her book, *Education on the Dalton Plan*, was published in 1922, and within six months of publication it was translated into fourteen languages. During the 1920s and 1930s, she traveled by invitation to such places as England, Japan, Russia, China, Chile, Denmark, and Germany, lecturing on her educational philosophy.

Before discussing the philosophy and implementation of The Dalton Plan, it is necessary to place it within its historical context. Helen Parkhurst was working during the heyday of the progressive movement in education. In New York City experimental schools such as the Lincoln School and the Children's School (the Walden School) were taking root. Parkhurst, therefore, was not an isolated visionary but rather a part of the progressive movement.[9]

Moreover, Helen Parkhurst formulated The Dalton Plan during a time when many educators were concerned with attending to the needs of the child, rather than fitting the child into the existing structure. In this way, Parkhurst was also the beneficiary of the coming of age of psychology as a discipline.

Helen Parkhurst was, above all, concerned with providing students with a better way to learn, a way which would permit them "to pursue and organize their studies their own way."[10] She desired to create

> a community environment to supply experiences to free the native impulses and interests of each individual of the group. Any impediments in the way of native impulses

---

[7]Marilyn Moss Feldman, ed. *Dalton School: A Book of Memories* (New York: Dalton School, 1979).

[8]Interview with Mrs. Nora Hodges, January 24, 1979.

[9]For a more detailed account see Cremin, *The Transformation of the School*, pp. 274-91.

[10]Helen Parkhurst, *Education on the Dalton Plan* (London: G. Bell and Sons, 1927), p. 15.

prevent the release of pupil energy. It is not the creation of pupil energy, but its release and use that is the problem of education.[11]

The guiding principles of her plan were freedom and cooperation. By freedom, Parkhurst intended the student to work free from

> interruption...upon any subject in which he is absorbed, because when interested he is mentally keener, more alert, and more capable of mastering any difficulty that may arise in the course of his study.[12]

To this end she abolished bells, for she was also cognizant of the fact that students acquire knowledge at their own rate and that they must have time to learn thoroughly. As Parkhurst dramatically suggests, "Freedom is taking one's own time. To take someone else's time is slavery."[13]

By cooperation, Parkhurst meant "the interaction of group life."[14] Concerned with preparing students to live in a democracy, she attempted to create an environment where there would be maximum cooperation and interaction between student and student, students and teachers. Believing that "education is a co-operative task,"[15] she set out to implement her principle through the work problem:

> Under the Dalton Laboratory Plan we place the work problem squarely before him (the student), indicating the standard which has to be attained. After that he is allowed to tackle it as he thinks fit in his own way and at his own speed. Responsibility for the result will develop not only his latent intellectual powers, but also his judgment and

---

[11]Helen Parkhurst as quoted in Evelyn Dewey, *The Dalton Laboratory Plan* (New York: E.P. Dutton and Co., 1922), p. 136.

[12]Parkhurst, *Education on the Dalton Plan*, p. 16.

[13]Ibid.

[14]Ibid.

[15]Ibid., p. 19.

character.[16]

Students, in September, would be confronted with the year's work in each subject. They would be required to discuss their plans of action with their teachers, for it was essential to Parkhurst that both students and teachers perceive their tasks. Later, students might discuss their plans with their fellow students; they might modify their plans on peer recommendations; they might even abandon their plans and start over. Students would have participated, nevertheless, in planning their studies with both faculty and peers, interacting with the community in a spirit of cooperation.

In addition to planning, cooperation could be achieved through student activities, such as clubs and committees, and the House system, the latter a particular Dalton phenomenon. Helen Parkhurst conceived of the House, particularly in the High School, as the arrangement of the student population into advisory groups representing all four grades and meeting four times per week for a total period of ninety minutes with a teacher-advisor.

House meetings might consist of students planning their work with their advisors, discussing problems of scheduling appointments with teachers, or perhaps an assembly as a group in order to discharge their responsibility to the rest of the community. House discussions might approach the more personal level, too. Student attitudes, habits and experiences might be considered by the group, for they have a definite bearing on community life within the school. Thus House would foster the spirit of cooperation among students; however, it would also serve to develop the qualities of independence and social awareness.[17]

Other important components of The Dalton Plan are the contract system and the assignment. In the Children's University School and, then, in the early stages of the Dalton School, the curriculum was divided into "jobs" encompassing twenty day time-periods. Students "contracted" for

---

[16]Ibid., p. 18.

[17]Helen Parkhurst, "Report of the Dalton School to the Commission on the Relation of School and College" (New York: Dalton School Archives, 1937), p. 5 (mimeographed).

their tasks and signed a contract to the effect.[18] Students' tasks appeared as the assignment—"an outline of the contract job with all its parts."[19]

To free the children, to assist their growth in independence and responsibility, large blocks of time were set aside each morning from nine to twelve o'clock called lab time. Each teacher had a lab and students would be expected to utilize the resources of their teachers in order to help them fulfill their contracts. Lab could either be a group or individual experience; lab rooms were stocked with textbooks and "adult books," as well, to facilitate learning.

Student progress was recorded by the graph method. There were, at the beginning, four graphs: an instructor's laboratory graph, a pupil's contract graph, a house graph, and an attendance graph. The instructor's graph was posted in each lab and students would mark off how many units of work they accomplished, twenty units being equal to one assignment. Subject teachers and students alike could use the instructor's graph to measure progress; for the teacher it served as a means of determining when a "conference" might be called in which a group of students reaching the same level might come together to discuss certain problems they held in common. For students, these graphs allowed them to measure their achievement in relation to the group as a whole. The pupils' contract graph permitted them to record their progress in all subjects and became known, later on, as the unit card for, like the instructor's graph, it contained space for twenty units divided into four sections for each week of the twenty-day period. The house graph emphasized the entire number of units of work completed and contained a space for individual house members to record their progress. This served mainly as a tool for the House Advisor. The attendance graph was posted on a bulletin board, accessible to students. It was the students' responsibility to record the time they arrived each morning.

Teachers under Parkhurst's plan were referred to as "specialists," for she believed that they knew their subject matter intimately. Training and credentials, however, were not important. In fact, one of her most eminent and talented teachers, Elizabeth Seeger, author of *The Pageant of Chinese*

---

[18]The younger children were expected to sign contracts. This was not so in the High School.

[19]Parkhurst, *Education on the Dalton Plan*, p. 47.

History, only completed high school. To her credit, Helen Parkhurst saw the teacher,

> not as a peddler of facts, but one who helps to recreate personality. Every child has a very definite personality, but a great deal of work needs to be done on all personalities. It takes time to make adjustments. It is necessary for us not only to extend our own personalities, but to consider the school a garden where many personalities are to be encouraged.[20]

Flexibility, then, was the keystone of the plan. Conferences were called as needed. Classes met, too, as needed, and consisted of grade meetings to discuss problems common to that age group. The school during Helen Parkhurst's time exuded a quality of informality, spur of the moment decision-making, enormous energy, high-level engagement on the part of both faculty and students, and the element of surprise. Harold Thorne, a former teacher, now deceased, was fond of saying, "You could come back to your classroom on Monday and someone else would be teaching there."[21]

Andre Malraux once said that artists theorize about what they would like to do but they do what they can do. Helen Parkhurst's Dalton Laboratory Plan, as she conceived it, was far from perfect. Former students complained of lack of structure, of conferences called without warning, of the disruption of precious time needed to complete projects. Teachers had to be reeducated in Dalton ways. Often, because of emphasis on process, they were insecure with regard to curriculum. For the student to realize his/her potential as an individual and to be a contributing member of a community remained a problem largely unsettled.

The Dalton Plan flourished in the lower grades, particularly from four through eight. Because of college requirements, it was not introduced in the High School until 1933, when Dalton became part of a group of independent schools participating in the Eight Year Experiment.

---

[20]Helen Parkhurst, "Lecture at Caxton Hall" (New York: Dalton School Archives, 1926), p. 9 (mimeographed).

[21]Interview with Georgia C. Rice, January 26, 1979.

Helen Parkhurst founded a school with a particular philosophy, a special environment where teachers had lab rooms and classrooms and educational jargon indigenous to the institution. But perhaps Parkhurst's greatest contribution to education and the *raison d'etre* of her school was her emphasis on process rather than product. She saw the Dalton Plan as "a vehicle for the curriculum, i.e., a new way of school living, permitting children to acquire flexible habits to put behind ideas."[22] She sought to instill in her students "good habits" because she realized the necessity of being able to adjust to new situations with facility as the primary principle of living. She believed that she was creating an environment in her school which would allow her students to make "adjustments and do things in terms of principle...to get the right mental habits for life."[23] As Helen Parkhurst stated in her Caxton Hall Lecture,

> the trouble with the education given to us in the past is that it really was not a preparation for the particular kind of living that we are enjoying today. Statesmen, teachers, all professions are baffled by problems that we face but do not solve. We must have flexible individuals in the future, who can do their tasks which we, in our ignorance, are unable even to discern today.[24]

Granted this description of The Dalton Plan, one might usefully locate it within the larger context of the progressive education movement. As noted earlier, Parkhurst was not an isolated visionary but rather one of many people who established child-centered day schools in New York City. Harold Rugg and Ann Schumacher, in their book, *The Child-Centered School*, place this movement in a national context, listing such schools as the Organic School in Fairhope, Alabama, founded by Marietta Johnson in 1907; the Park School in Baltimore, Maryland, founded by Eugene Smith in 1912; the Oak Lane Country Day School in Philadelphia, Pennsylvania, founded by Francis M. Froelicher in 1916. They also mention that during these years before World War I, "Carleton Washburne began his experimen-

---

[22]Parkhurst, "Lecture at Caxton Hall," p. 5.
[23]Ibid., p. 9.
[24]Ibid., p. 10.

tation in the practical individualization of instruction in Winnetka, Illinois,"[25] within a large, public setting.

Parkhurst's Dalton Laboratory Plan is original in its language only; it is a synthesis of the ideas of leading progressive educators of her day; and, as will be demonstrated, perhaps had its origin in the "individual system" of Carleton Washburne. Parkhurst, herself, in giving credence to her ideas, credits John Dewey with having directly inspired her. As a medieval scholastic might refer to Aristotle as authority, so Helen Parkhurst invokes John Dewey. She makes the connection easy for her reader by demonstrating that the second principle of The Dalton Plan, cooperation or the interaction of group life, as having been taken from Dewey's *Democracy and Education* and quotes the passage for emphasis.[26]

Her chapter in *Education on the Dalton Plan* entitled "Inception of the Dalton Plan" is particularly relevant to this discussion, both for what is included and for what is omitted. Helen Parkhurst credits Edgar Swift's book, *Mind in the Making*, as profoundly influencing her, maintains that she owed her "first conception of educational laboratories" to it; she quotes extensively from this text on such matters as working "with the students, inspiring them to delve into things for themselves."[27]

She continues to explain her "philosophical evolutionary process" with a brief allusion to her experience in Italy with Maria Montessori, and then moves on to mention Frederic Burk, who made it possible for her to make "a practical test of her laboratory plan upon a selected group of one hundred children, between the ages of nine and twelve."[28]

I believe that in order to understand fully the origins of The Dalton Plan, we should look to a name Parkhurst omitted, Carleton Washburne, a man who became associated with the "individual system," or the Winnetka Plan, and whose schema bears resemblance to Helen Parkhurst's Dalton Plan.

It is interesting to note that both have in common as a mentor Frederic Burk. Lawrence A. Cremin, in *The Transformation of the School*,

---

[25]Harold Rugg and Ann Schumacher, *The Child-Centered School* (New York: Arno Press, 1969), p. 51.

[26]See Parkhurst, *Education on the Dalton Plan*, p. 20.

[27]Ibid., p. 10.

[28]Ibid., p. 14.

describes Burk's work at the San Francisco Normal School:

> President Frederic Burk had begun as early as 1912 to
> redesign the curriculum of the model elementary school to
> allow greater freedom for each of the 700 students to
> progress through his studies at his own particular pace.
> Each child was given a copy of the course of study for
> each subject on his program. Class recitations were
> abandoned, as were daily assignments. Provision was made
> for testing and promoting pupils as soon as the work
> outlined for any grade in any subject was completed.[29]

Cremin traces the outcome of Burk's "individual system" as culminating in
the work of three people: Willard W. Beatty, Carleton Washburne, and
Helen Parkhurst.

For the purpose of this discussion, it is necessary to look at
Carleton Washburne vis-à-vis Helen Parkhurst. Washburne worked, as he
stated in his book *Winnetka: The History and Significance of an Educational
Experiment*, "under the aegis of Frederic Burk for five years." Then in May
of 1919, he assumed the position of Superintendent of the Winnetka Public
Schools. There,

> in 1919...what came to be known as the Winnetka educa-
> tional system had its origin. The source was three
> streams—the educational desires of Winnetka, Burk's work
> in San Francisco, and my own early experiences followed
> by the rigorous training under Burk. Therefore all three
> influences merged into one continuous stream.[30]

Washburne's "individual system" and Parkhurst's Dalton Laboratory Plan
have much in common. Both are based on the ideas that the child should
progress at its own pace, and both use the method of individualized

---

[29]Cremin, *The Transformation of the School*, pp. 295-96.

[30]Carleton W. Washburne and Sidney P. Marland, Jr., *Winnetka: The
History and Significance of an Educational Experiment* (Englewood Cliffs,
N.J.: Prentice-Hall, 1963), p. 14.

instruction to this end. Both emphasize the idea of group life through projects, student government, clubs, and committees. Both have similar content in their projects; for example, Greek Olympic Games which have become institutionalized at Dalton were part of the curriculum for fifth graders in Winnetka. Both have some standardized form of measurement for student progress: Parkhurst used unit cards or progress charts; Washburne used goal cards. And both have systematic approaches to individualized work: Parkhurst used assignments that followed a particular set structure, while Washburne used "specially prepared individual progress materials."

Obviously, contemporaries of both had difficulty discussing the differences between the plans set forth by Washburne and Parkhurst—so much so that Washburne addressed this problem in a footnote in his book:

> The "Winnetka Plan" has often been confused with the "Dalton Plan." The "Dalton Plan" first worked out in her Children's University School in New York by Helen Parkhurst, was tried in the public high school in Dalton, Massachusetts, beginning in 1920. It had, at first one thing in common with our work in Winnetka. It did, during the early years, provide the individual progress of the children. I shall not attempt to describe the Dalton Plan—Miss Parkhurst has done so fully in books and periodicals, with translations in several languages. It had many merits and it had very wide vogue, especially in the British Commonwealth (its first fame was in England), in the Netherlands, in the early days of the USSR, and in the Orient. It differed markedly from the work in Winnetka in that it was never characterized by research, by the preparation of self-instructive teaching materials, by the scientific construction of curriculum ("The Dalton Plan," Miss Parkhurst said, "is a vehicle for any kind of curriculum."), or by techniques for group and creative activities.[31]

I certainly would agree with Washburne that his Winnetka Plan was far more "scientific" than Parkhurst's pedagogy, although perhaps I would

---

[31]Ibid., pp. 152-53.

substitute systematic or rational for the word, scientific.

It still remains a mystery as to why Parkhurst made no mention of Carleton Washburne's work. In fact, in a letter to Lawrence A. Cremin, shortly before she died, she protested his linking her with the Burk-Washburne strain and emphatically stated that Maria Montessori was her teacher, in every respect.

In the final analysis, however, the degree to which her thinking was original matters not a whit to the institution Parkhurst founded. Her genius lay in her ability to merchandise existing ideas, to publicize, and popularize. Like the *philosophes* of the eighteenth century who publicized and popularized the scientific revolution of the seventeenth century, Helen Parkhurst publicized and popularized the strain of individualized instruction, an important current in progressive education. She was not original, but she was effective as a woman in education with a vision that became a reality with the creation of the Dalton School.

3

EDUCATION ON THE DALTON PLAN:
THE WAY IT WAS (1919–1942)

Helen Parkhurst's personal style set the tone of the Dalton School from the very beginning. A forceful, creative individual, she inspired great devotion—in some, even a fierce loyalty—on the part of her staff, students, and parents. Her authoritarian, paternalistic, nonrational mode of administration was tolerated by the school community precisely because she was viewed as a great educator and a formidable individual. As will become evident, Helen Parkhurst went about the business of deciding upon educational philosophy and its implementation, expansion of the physical plant, and financial matters undaunted by guidelines and decisions made by her board of trustees. As one former trustee and admirer stated, "You might decide something at a board meeting, but she wouldn't do it." Parkhurst truly believed that the Dalton School was her creation and, in the end, was inextricably connected with the institution she had created.

Although the Dalton School had been in existence before 1929, records are sparse and intermittent for this early period. Thus, for our purposes, the history of the school will begin in 1929, when the physical plant was moved to its present location at 108 East 89th Street, and a board of trustees was created which kept recorded minutes. By this time coeducation had been phased out of the High School, and enrollment was estimated at 383 students.[1] The building at 89th Street was under-utilized from the very beginning, for enrollment during the Parkhurst years never reached 500 students. Students from these early years constantly cite the unusual amount of space in which to play and the great freedom of movement within the building. The truth of the matter was that Dalton opened its new doors during the onslaught of the Depression, and for many years thereafter, suffered, as did many other independent schools, from underenrollment.

---

[1] It is important to keep in mind that the Dalton School of today has an enrollment of over 1200 students. Thus, it has more than tripled in size since the early years. This increase in size has had significant effects, which will be discussed in subsequent chapters.

Parkhurst, however, managed to attract a small if steady stream of applicants to Dalton through her speaking engagements, publications, and personal contacts. Many parents chose Dalton because of Parkhurst's educational philosophy. Once a child from a multi-sibling family entered the school, the others were not far behind. One informant related that Parkhurst, while visiting her mother to discuss her older brother, saw her, age two-and-a-half, toddling around the house and announced, "Send that child to school"—whereupon a class of preprimary students was created with the two-and-a-half year old as its first member. Dalton became a school for children of the professional class, with a well balanced religious distribution through the Middle School. Many of the Protestant families, however, withdrew their children from Dalton's more permissive atmosphere after the eighth grade, to exchange it for more traditional modes of education.[2] Ultimately, to counter the loss of male students going off to boarding schools, Parkhurst declared the High School the exclusive province of female Dalton students.

The school attracted children of people actively engaged in the arts and in education (many of whom were placed on scholarship) and also children who had physical disabilities. Thus early on, Dalton became known as a "motherly institution," precisely because it attended to individual differences well beyond learning styles.[3]

The Dalton School achieved a great amount of national prominence through a unique opportunity presented to Helen Parkhurst: participation in the Eight Year Study. In 1930, the Progressive Education Association, meeting at its annual convention in Washington, D.C., posed the question, "How can the high school improve its service to American youth?"[4] A Commission on the Relation of School and College was formed under the leadership of Wilford M. Aiken, consisting of twenty-six members "concerned with the revision of the work of the secondary school and eager to find some way to remove the obstacle of rigid prescription."[5] By 1932, an experimental solution was found through a plan which allowed coopera-

---

[2]Interview with Elizabeth Steinway Chapin, February 9, 1979.

[3] Interview with Frank Carnabuci, September 29, 1990.

[4]Wilford M. Aiken, *The Story of the Eight-Year Study* (New York and London: Harper and Brothers, 1942), p. 1.

[5]Ibid., p. 2.

tion between a select group of twenty-eight[6] schools and the colleges and universities permitting the schools to be

> released from the usual subjects and unit requirements for college admission for a period of five years, beginning with the class entering college in 1936. Practically all accredited colleges and universities agreed to this plan. Relatively few colleges require (d) candidates to take College Entrance Board Examinations.[7]

Dalton School psychologist, Dr. Genevieve L. Coy, served on three subcommittees of Records and Reports established by the Commission; Dr. Hilda Taba, Dalton School curriculum coordinator, served as an associate on the Evaluation Staff of the Commission, headed by Dr. Ralph W. Tyler.

The Eight Year Study created a very exciting time for the Dalton School community. Former staff members were eloquent about this period in the school's history. Former students, too, note an excitement generated by participating in an educational experiment in which staff, students, and parents frequently came together to discuss the purpose of education and to speculate on what should be taught. Giles et al. characterize this feeling as "the adventure of living"[8] and, undoubtedly, the Dalton community generated an atmosphere similar to the feeling of adventure in embarking upon previously uncharted waters.

The Eight Year Experiment for Dalton, however, when placed in proper perspective, might be viewed as an extension of Parkhurst's Dalton Plan into the High School. Curriculum had to be reorganized in an attempt to reflect a particular philosophy of education that was already present in the Primary and Middle Schools:

> (1) the development of many sides of the child's na-
> ture—intellectual, emotional, esthetic, spiritual;

---

[6]Later, two more schools in California were added.

[7]Aiken, p. 12.

[8]H.H. Giles, S.P. McCutchen, and A.N. Zechiel, *Exploring the Curriculum* (New York and London: Harper and Brothers, 1942), p. 289.

(2) provision for individual differences;

(3) the development of that self-discipline in the pupil which makes it possible for him to use freedom;

(4) the growth of an active appreciation of, and concern for,the needs and achievements of other individuals and peoples.[9]

The philosophy of the High School incorporated these precepts, placing a strong emphasis on "appreciation of individual differences" and "social awareness" so that the purposes of a Dalton education was to prepare the student to live in a democratic society. Curriculum, Parkhurst stated, should not be presented as subjects in "water-tight compartments" but rather, integrated, cutting across subject lines ...which might help the student orient herself towards large problems of the present world."[10] School objectives were defined as:

(1) the development on the part of the student of a personally formulated and cherished outlook on life. This is the over-arching objective of the program, and it is, finally, the *integrating force for the individual*.

(2) the development of intellectual powers: generalization, consistency and persistency in thinking, planning and through an attack upon problems; transfer of ideas from one field of action to another, etc.

(3) the development of intellectual tools; basic concepts and information in significant areas of knowledge, ability to read with purpose, ability to discriminate in reading and in observation, facility in oral and written expression, etc.

---

[9]Helen Parkhurst, "Report of the Dalton School to the Commission on the Relation of School and College" (New York: Dalton School Archives, 1937), p. 1 (mimeographed).

[10]Ibid., pp. 1–2.

(4) the development of a self-awareness that leads to satisfying and joyful living. This is the over-arching objective *for the student*, though perhaps never formulated. It will be realized through location of interests, pursuit of interests, understanding of self—through social relationships, plan of imagination in all areas of school activity, etc.[11]

The curriculum was organized so that students would "form a unified point of view on some of the problems of modern life"[12] and the technique of selecting large problems for students to work on was adopted in order for them to better comprehend their environment. The course of study in the Dalton High School for four years was:

Grade 9: Life in New York City, considered as a metropolitan community.

Grade 10: The Political, Economic, and Cultural Trends which have given character and differentiation to Life in the United States today.

Grade 11: The Impact of European Culture on Our Life Today.

Grade 12: Outstanding, International Problems and America's Relation to them.[13]

Ninth grade students, in additions to their prescribed course of studies, were also obliged to care for infants during two weeks in the fall and two weeks in the spring of the freshman year. This program, known as "the nursery," grew out of an inspiration Parkhurst had when a close friend and trustee of the school became pregnant. Helen Parkhurst decided to develop a course in which students cared for babies from disadvantaged

---

[11]Ibid., p. 2.
[12]Ibid., p. 5.
[13]Ibid.

families in order "to make human biology more meaningful."[14] The program began in the spring of 1932[15] on a voluntary basis, open to all high school students. By 1936, it became an integral part of the high school biology program for ninth graders. In addition to caring for the babies, students were responsible for picking up and delivering the children home in the school car. One informant interviewed stated that she learned more about life in her surrounding community from these home visits than any other school experience. She was particularly impressed with the treatment of the infant as dictated by its socioeconomic circumstances and cultural background. After carefully nurturing the child at school, she was shocked to see it was fed mashed spaghetti, meat sauce, and diluted wine at home.

Students in the nursery also studied such topics as digestion, food, diet, disease, bacteria, reproduction, and heredity. Trips to places such as Borden's Milk Plant and New York Hospital were also arranged. A registered nurse supervised the Nursery and a physician visited daily to examine the babies. This program remained as an integral part of the freshman year through 1956.

The impact of the Eight Year Study on the Dalton School was candidly assessed by Dr. Ralph W. Tyler in a letter to Professor Bode, a member of the Directing Committee, in which he stated that the data on Dalton were far more complete than for any other school in the Eight Year Study, and that "achievement of the girls in the new high school program is outstanding."[16] On reading tests, Dalton high school seniors were found to be superior to the average college sophomore; on writing samples, seniors were found to be superior to the average college juniors. After having attended a government assembly, Dr. Tyler concluded that the students exhibited an impressive verbal ability, that the "girls speak as effectively as the ordinary college graduate."[17] He also found evidence of growth of critical thinking and the easy transfer of ideas into new areas. Dr. Tyler felt

---

[14]Helen Parkhurst, "Motherhood Training, High School Nursery" (New York: Dalton School Archives, n.d.), p. 1.

[15]Evidence conflicts as to the exact date; however, correspondence points to 1932.

[16]Board of Trustees, "Minutes (New York: Dalton School, 1937), p. 360.

[17]Ibid., pp. 360–61.

the outstanding features of Dalton's program were that teachers worked together cooperatively, taking advantage of the city to augment the curriculum, that high school girls learned about human behavior and family problems through working in the nursery school division, that there was, in general, greater coordination of educational efforts between family and home. In closing, Dr. Tyler concluded, "such a significant contribution to American education ought to be continued."[18]

Dr. Tyler was an enthusiastic supporter of what he saw happening at Dalton and was an inspiration to the staff. Giles et al. and Aiken, however, place the Dalton developments in a larger context so that one comes away with the understanding that what might be unique and exciting to the Dalton community was somewhat commonplace among the participants in the study. Core or integrated curriculum design were learning strategies adopted by the majority of schools participating in the study. Dalton, however, was cited by the evaluators as particularly outstanding in its community studies through the implementation of field trips[19] and in its articulation between all fields and grade levels.[20] Aiken was impressed with a three day conference held at Dalton on vocations in which students, parents and teachers participated.[21]

How did the students feel? In a document prepared by Helen Parkhurst entitled "Working Together," she includes excerpts from the text of a three day Parents Education Conference held at school on the topic "As We Have Grown." Students questioned by Dr. Alice Keliher, Chairman of the Commission on Human Relations, and Dr. Constance Warren, President of Sarah Lawrence College, in order to determine some of the values inherent in a Dalton education, stated that the school made them aware of themselves—they were cognizant of the need "to collect their own evidence" and "not accept knowledge passively." Freedom, responsibility, and comprehension of the process whereby knowledge is obtained were frequently mentioned both in this document and by former students. Personal growth, social consciousness and the spirit of cooperation were also cited as qualities gleaned from the learning experience at Dalton.

---

[18]Ibid., p. 362.
[19]Giles et al., p. 136.
[20]Ibid., p. 239.
[21]Aiken, p. 66.

The Eight Year Experiment instituted in 1933 lasted until 1940. It made a significant impact on the Dalton community and influenced the course of studies in the High School for many years thereafter. In addition, policy towards college admissions was established as Charlotte Keefe Durham, then director of the High School, noted in a letter: "I never sent a mark to colleges and, as you know, many of you were welcomed into excellent colleges."[22] For many years after the Eight Year Experiment was terminated, grading continued to be minimized and it was not until the sixties that it again became an issue with faculty members, students, and parents.

Helen Parkhurst and her staff worked tirelessly during this experimental period to perfect their notion of Dalton's philosophy of education and to implement it in the curriculum. She delegated the running of the High School to Charlotte Keefe Durham; however, Mrs. Durham notes that when Parkhurst was Headmistress "she was central and final in its management—very few ideas came from the faculty."[23] She characterizes Parkhurst as "a benevolent, creative, autocrat,"[24] who "cared passionately about freedom for children and went to great lengths to originate plans for that and student responsibility, e.g., the nursery, Dalton Plan."[25]

That Helen Parkhurst was enmeshed in every aspect of school life was an understatement. She would visit the homes of their students, befriend parents, and open previously untapped channels of communication between school and home. A believer in conferences as an effective vehicle of communication, she held many during her administration in which students, parents and faculty participated. A three day Parents Education Conference held in May, 1938, dealt with studying the needs of the children and their education "to acquaint parents with the kind of work and activities the students are engaged in throughout the school."[26] During one meeting, students presented their views of what sort of teacher they preferred; parents expressed their views of what sort of teacher they would like to have as their child's instructor. Teachers reported on what kind of parents they

---

[22] Correspondence with Charlotte Keefe Durham, February 22, 1979.
[23] Ibid.
[24] Ibid.
[25] Ibid.
[26] *The Daltonian* (New York: Dalton School Archives, May 20, 1938).

would "appreciate."

    Helen Parkhurst also was fond of appearing at student assemblies to discuss the Dalton Plan. She would also call students at random to her office as individuals or in groups to discuss personal or communal concerns. In addition, she instituted a reporting system, not just for parents of Dalton students, but for nurses and governesses who were concerned with the welfare of their charges. Parkhurst's commitment to the school community was contagious. Parents, too, became so involved with the education of their children that one was moved to write a letter to the student newspaper testifying to that effect:

> Being a parent of a daughter who has been practically brought up in Miss Parkhurst's school, I feel it almost a sacred duty to follow the activities of the school and the principles it teaches. I have watched with pleasure the splendid progress of my child in her studies and in her general development and I often ask myself what are some of the outstanding characteristics that my child has been imbued with through her contact with her teachers and her superiors. One of the most striking of these, I would say, is the clear development of her own logical thinking and her persistent demand for logical reasoning on the part of her parents, also.
>
>   A Dalton Admirer[27]

    The most telling portrait of Parkhurst, however, can be found through reading the minutes of the board of trustees and by interviewing former board members. What emerges is a picture of an administrator who did as she pleased, regardless of what the board mandated. She was, of course, supported by certain board members who were close personal friends, such as Helen Parkhurst's patroness, Mrs. W. Murray Crane, and Mrs. Evangeline Stokowska. Mrs. Stokowska often accompanied Parkhurst on trips both school-related and personal; she also provided financial support when additional funds were necessary. The antique, renaissance-style

---

[27]*The Daltonian*, October 30, 1930.

cabinets that once graced the second floor corridors were said to have come from Stokowska's apartment; likewise, the elaborate gold threaded drapes that were transformed into angels' costumes for the Christmas Pageant. Helen Parkhurst also received support on the board, first, from Benjamin Buttenwieser, a wealthy and prominent member of the New York German-Jewish community who had an immense respect for education and believed in Parkhurst's ideas; then, when Buttenwieser left to join the Navy, from his wife, Helen, a lawyer. Parkhurst also commanded the loyalty of trustee Lloyd Goodrich, art historian and curator of the Whitney Museum, whose son was the recipient of a scholarship. It is alleged that those members who forcefully opposed her were pressured until they resigned for either "reasons of health" or "business responsibilities." Parkhurst was able to manipulate the board successfully until the advent of Mr. Richardson Wood as president. Then her style of leadership led to her undoing.

As stated in the minutes of the Board for September 26, 1929, the responsibilities of the head of the school were as follows:

> The Head of School shall have full charge of the education-
> al policy of the school and its administration, for both of
> which she shall be responsible to the Board of Trust-
> ees.[28]

The head of the school was also mandated to "regulate the course of study, school sessions and vacations, admission, suspension and expulsion of pupils."[29] Only later, in 1936, did the board act to curb the power of the headmistress by creating a small educational advisory board consisting of three teachers, Miss Keefe, Miss Seeger, and Mrs. Mukerji, to act in concert with Helen Parkhurst on matters concerning educational policy "and to accept responsibility of maintaining budget limits established by the Board."[30] Any payments made by the school had to have the signatures of Parkhurst and two of the three teachers on the advisory board. These three teachers, however, were close to Parkhurst and sources interviewed stated that they were likely "to do her bidding."

---

[28] Board of Trustees, Minutes, September 26, 1929, p. 5.

[29] Ibid., p. 7.

[30] Board of Trustees, Minutes, October, 1936, p.3.

There is much evidence that Helen Parkhurst acted with calculated insouciance in regard to money matters. In 1937, she spent $250.00 on publicity photographs of the school, although unauthorized to do so by the board. She cavalierly stated that the PTA would pay the bill. The board, however, objected, stating that the PTA was not responsible for the debt and that Parkhurst should pay for the photographs herself. Yet, the PTA willingly paid the bill, for Parkhurst was quite successful in her ability to coopt the parents.

While Helen Parkhurst may have carefully thought out her educational philosophy, she certainly did not devote the same amount of meticulous planning to school policy. A particular example of shoddy planning was the infamous merger with the Todhunter School in 1939, "a conservative, fashionable school for girls—totally unrelated to Dalton ideals."[31] According to several sources, the Todhunter School presented a number of desirable elements to Parkhurst. First and foremost, it had $17,000 in its building fund which might be added to Dalton's construction fund. It also had Mrs. Franklin Roosevelt on its board, Bernard Baruch's daughter as a student, and a population drawn from wealthy East Side Protestant families. Dalton teachers were not consulted about the merger nor was the board consulted about Parkhurst's plan until she had informally mustered support from some board members.

"The merger," states Charlotte Keefe Durham, "was a disaster. Confusion and questionable financial plans followed from both sides."[32] Few Todhunter students came to Dalton; those who did left the following year. Parkhurst, nevertheless, managed to keep the $17,000 from the Todhunter building fund and applied it the following year to her fund to expand the 89th Street building.

Yet another incident of thoughtlessness and dictatorial management on the part of Helen Parkhurst was her "New Milford Experiment" or "City and Country," as one trustee referred to this scheme. Apparently no one involved seems to know exactly how it came about, what its purpose was, when it was first implemented and how it was financed—although there is much speculation, especially in regard to the latter. There is, however, much agreement on the fact that the site was chosen because Helen

---

[31]Charlotte Keefe Durham correspondence.
[32]Ibid.

Parkhurst had a country house in New Milford, Connecticut.

The first mention of New Milford is found in an editorial in *The Daltonian* on December 1, 1937, entitled "Integration of Work and Play." It comments favorably on Helen Parkhurst's notion of obtaining a small house in the country where some members of the high school might go for a week and combine academic studies with nature studies and winter sports. Students interviewed who had participated in New Milford were unclear as to why they were there. One viewed it as "a lark"; another stated it to be "the most miserable experience of my life." *The Daltonian* of February 28, 1941, reported that on March 1st, students from the junior and senior classes and the faculty would go to New Milford for one month in which they would devote their weekdays to academic studies and spend their weekends taking field trips. Apparently the students were boarded in dormitories and fed in a communal mess hall. It was thought that these facilities were constructed to house city children who might have to be evacuated because of the war. As to the ownership of the property, one informant speculated that Parkhurst had purchased the site through remortgaging the 89th Street building. There is no evidence to support this latter piece of speculation. It is a fact, however, that Parkhurst could not account for the sum of more than $40,000 over the budget, according to board minutes. According to another informant, the faculty who participated in this experiment were "good sports"; however, it was felt that there was an undercurrent of resentment for the authoritarian, insensitive manner in which it was implemented. Indeed, it must have been quite difficult for faculty members with families to absent themselves from home for a full month.

Parkhurst's building expansion program, which she undertook in 1940, illustrates her lack of concern for board approval and perhaps serves to underscore her feeling that the school was hers to direct as she saw fit. Parkhurst decided to implement a plan to build additions to the east and west wings of the school. Without giving the board notice, she sent letters to parents asking for contributions, the percentage to be determined by the amount of tuition paid to support her program. Ultimately she did obtain board approval but only after she procured loans from two parents totalling the full amount of the projected expenditure.

Helen Parkhurst's achilles heel was money. She raised it successfully but spent it imprudently. In 1938, she reported to the board in her annual message that the cash deficit of 1929 had been completely eliminated. Yet, in 1940, because of lack of funds, the faculty had to pitch in and donate a percentage of their salaries to the school to prevent the staff from being cut. Two years later, in 1942, after declaring a financial deficit of $91,764.65, the school went into bankruptcy. Where did the money go? Many informants interviewed stated that Parkhurst used school funds for personal gain and that she whimsically granted scholarships. Whatever the case, the climax leading to the inevitable denouement occurred in 1942, when the board under the presidency of Mr. Richardson Wood, editor of *Fortune Magazine*, investigated the school's finances. Concurrently, the faculty, particularly in the high school, split into two factions. Many of its newer members voiced strong opposition to Parkhurst's dictatorial approach in determining academic policy. The schism unleashed such passion that for years thereafter, one loyal Parkhurst supporter, Dora Downes, refused to speak to members of the opposition.

According to board minutes, during a private meeting on April 30, 1942, in which Helen Parkhurst, Richardson Wood, Charles D. Hilles, and Stanley Isaacs were present, Parkhurst agreed to resign. Subsequently, a formal announcement of her resignation was made in a board meeting on May 5th. A letter written by Helen Parkhurst tendering her resignation was accepted by the board and her contract was to be terminated as of June, 1942.

There is much evidence to support the proposition that Helen Parkhurst did not accept her fate lightly. One faculty member reports that Parkhurst, in an attempt to quell the faculty revolt, called an assembly of high school students, locked the faculty out, told the students not to go to classes, assured them that no one would fail, and promised to sign the diplomas of graduating seniors.[33] She also contacted former board members and powerful parents to muster support. During the board meeting of May 13th, thirty-five telegrams and notes from parents were delivered to the chairman, expressing opposition to or disappointment in Parkhurst's resignation. The most pathetic series of events, however, were those that involved students being called into Parkhurst's office to be confronted by the once powerful headmistress, now begging them to go home and tell their parents, "I'm good, really I am."

One former trustee suggested that Parkhurst was guilty of financial "hanky panky." It is more than likely, however, that she viewed the school

---

[33]Incident related by Nora Hodges in an interview, January 24, 1979.

as her creation, her property, so that by the end of her administration she was incapable of distinguishing between what belonged to her and what belonged to the institution. Benjamin Buttenwieser, a trustee during Parkhurst's administration, said of her, "when she was on the ship she was captain." Her tragedy was that she failed to comprehend that the ship she commanded was only temporarily entrusted to her.

4

THE DURHAM ERA (1942–1960)

> In summary, I was educated by Helen Parkhurst—never
> repudiated her ideas but saw to it that they could function
> in an ordered way and I'm glad to say that the school
> survived as a result.[1]

Charlotte Anne Keefe Durham was, at a glance, the antithesis of Helen
Parkhurst. She was short, articulate, rational and organized; Parkhurst was
tall, surprisingly inarticulate, nonrational, and disorganized. Both were
intelligent and strong-willed, and had a love of the school necessary for the
survival of the institution.

Charlotte Durham had been considered by many informants to be
an extension of Helen Parkhurst. In her devotion to the Dalton Plan and in
her determination to save a financially floundering school she was, indeed,
following in Parkhurst's footsteps. As we shall see, however, the resemblance ends there.

Charlotte Durham came to Dalton in 1922, at the age of twenty-
two. She had one year of previous teaching experience at Brooklyn Heights
Seminary, a traditional school like Chapin. Its head, she stated in an
interview, was a "perfect horror." By chance, an employment agency sent
her to Dalton, by then located in two townhouses on West 72nd Street. She
was interviewed by Helen Parkhurst for over two hours in which she and
Parkhurst discussed a variety of subjects unrelated to education. Then, on
the spot, Parkhurst offered her a job teaching English. What particularly
impressed Mrs. Durham was the fact that the salary offered her by
Parkhurst was considerably more than she was making at Brooklyn Heights
Seminary.

Charlotte Durham came from a rather traditional background. She
was born and brought up in New London, Connecticut. She attended

---

[1] Charlotte Keefe Durham correspondence. Charlotte Anne Keefe became
Mrs. Charles Durham in 1948. Her husband was a Dalton parent.

Connecticut College, then an institution exclusively for women. She received a master's degree in English from Columbia University in New York City. Unlike most other members of the New England establishment, Charlotte Durham was a devout Roman Catholic.

As do most competent administrators, Charlotte Durham rose up through the ranks. Initially she was an English teacher dealing with children of various age levels. Helen Parkhurst became fond of her and appointed her liaison between the school and the outside world. This was an important function as Dalton received many visitors who wished to view a successfully functioning progressive school. She became an expert on the Dalton Plan, showed visitors around the school, and lectured on education on the Dalton Plan.

When Miss Parkhurst went to China, Mrs. Durham accompanied her. Together they founded a Dalton School. Mrs. Durham was subsequently sent to Ohio State University along with Elizabeth Seeger, an enormously talented teacher, to found a summer demonstration school. Later on, Helen Parkhurst sent her to Chile. Apparently the Chileans were not expecting Mrs. Durham; in fact, they were quite startled when she and her friend arrived to establish a Dalton School. This apparently was a Parkhurst trademark. However, with some financial aid from her parents and great personal determination, she established Dalton schools in Chile and Argentina. It is difficult to assess exactly what Charlotte Durham's administrative abilities were under Helen Parkhurst, considering that Parkhurst was loathe to relinquish control and invented titles to suit the moment. In fact, Mrs. Durham stated that Parkhurst once left the school to travel abroad and apparently left no one in charge. At some point, however, Charlotte Durham was made an "associate" of Miss Parkhurst. Then she became head of the High School. In that role she still continued to "interpret the Dalton Plan to outside people." In 1942, she assumed the leadership of the school.

How Mrs. Durham became headmistress has been variously interpreted. I feel most comfortable with Charlotte Durham's own account in which she states that Stanley Isaacs, the receiver of the school, approached her and requested that she become headmistress.[2] He and the

---

[2]According to Board Minutes, it was probable that she was first Acting Head.

board of trustees declared that if she declined the position, the school would be closed. She accepted "somewhat naively," and Miss Parkhurst was dismissed.[3]

Charlotte Durham inherited a bankrupt progressive school in New York City in 1942. Because of the war, there was a constant problem of shifting enrollment, and loss of faculty and board members to military service. Moreover, the school was torn by faculty factionalism with the older, established teachers tending to be pro-Parkhurst, and the younger, less established teachers tending to support the new regime. What the school had going for it, however, was an extremely valuable physical plant, an excellent location, a hard core of loyal, committed board members, such as Helen Buttenwieser and Stephen Duggan, and a creative, courageous headmistress. In a stroke of genius, Mrs. Durham engaged Dr. Ralph Tyler, Chairman of the Department of Education at the University of Chicago, to come to Dalton semi-monthly for two years and then monthly for an additional year.[4] His specific task was "to carry on educational research and study with the faculty." Dalton's association with Dr. Tyler began at the inception of the Eight Year Study. He and Miss Parkhurst, however, had little rapport. It has been suggested by Mrs. Durham that perhaps Miss Parkhurst and Dr. Tyler were too alike in personality and unwilling to bend to one another's ideas. Dr. Tyler has suggested that perhaps Miss Parkhurst had difficulty relating to strong males. Nevertheless, Dr. Tyler's presence at Dalton, said one informant, "took the minds of the teachers off their differences about the departure of Miss Parkhurst and brought them together over stimulating ideas." Dr. Tyler was to continue his consultancy through 1945 on a regular basis. After that, he had an occasional consulting job until he lost contact with the school during the Kittell and Barr administrations. Later, he would be engaged by headmaster Gardner P. Dunnan to evaluate the First Program.

Charlotte Durham's strategy worked. Tyler pulled the faculty together by engaging them as a group in examining their educational aims and values in an attempt to formulate a rational educational policy. His

---

[3]Or, her resignation was accepted.

[4]The actual amount of time Dr. Tyler spent at Dalton is difficult to ascertain since there is little agreement among informants, Dr. Tyler, and Board Minutes.

enthusiasm, vitality, knowledge, and support helped to unify the faculty and once again give it a sense of direction.

Charlotte Durham also engaged other consultants, particularly in the lower divisions of the school. In addition to Dr. Tyler, Dr. Dan Prescott and other members of the Department of Education from the University of Chicago worked with the faculty. Dr. Genevieve Coy, a member of the staff involved in psychological services, worked with High School personnel.

Often, the head of a school must function as both educator and business manager. Increasingly, Raymond Callahan notes, the business-oriented school superintendent eclipses the educational philosopher.[5] Rarely are both abilities integrated in one person. Charlotte Durham was most fortunate; she could attend to educational matters exclusively if she so desired. This was made possible because of the presence of Stanley Isaacs, the receiver of the school, who became its treasurer in 1945 at a salary of $3,000 per year. In February, 1941, the school had a total enrollment of 433 students: 276 students were paying full tuition; 159 were receiving scholarship aid. Against incredible odds, Isaacs balanced the budget while maintaining at least 25 percent of the student body on scholarship. Enrollment was increased by about 100 additional students. This was done gradually. Isaacs, along with other board members and Mrs. Durham, established a Dalton Fund, which he tapped for emergencies; with Charlotte Durham he established a pension plan for the faculty, encouraged fund-raising efforts, and worked out equitable solutions to problems posed by the unionized maintenance staff. An Alumni Association was established and the PTA continued its activities as it had under Parkhurst.

A school's reputation frequently rests with the quality of its faculty, and Dalton was no exception. Helen Parkhurst assembled an interesting and talented group of teachers; Charlotte Durham continued to do so. She took great pride in her artists-in-residence and encouraged talented people, working in their fields, to come to Dalton part-time as well as full-time. She operated on the premise that "the vitality of a school depends on the wise and creative use of teachers, talents, and energy." Among her artists were sculptress Rhys Caparn and painters Ruffino Tamayo and Vaclav Vytacil.

Unlike Helen Parkhurst, a former administrator noted, Charlotte

---

[5] Raymond Callahan, *Education and the Cult of Efficiency* (Chicago: University of Chicago Press, 1962).

Durham attempted to employ "well qualified people as well as imaginative, creative people." At board meetings she established the precedent of announcing the names of departing faculty members and those hired to replace them. She would describe carefully their reasons for departure, then note the educational backgrounds and teaching experience of new staff members. She seemed to be interested particularly in employing people who were specialists in their fields, had attended Ivy League schools, and taught in comparable independent schools. Significantly, few, if any, attended teachers colleges, except for those in the nursery division. She seemed to be partial to people who had graduated from English or French universities, especially for the High School. Many informants noted that because of her diverse faculty there were some highly charged flare-ups and disagreements. Indeed, faculty opinion, aired before students at High School government assemblies, was a constant source of amusement to the students and signalled the diverse opinions of the staff on such a minute issue as what color the smock, the uniform high school students wore, should be.

An adjective that keeps recurring in discussions about how Mrs. Durham orchestrated her staff and administered the school is "Jesuitical." She was firm; she had a small coterie of favorites; she would brook no nonsense. She did respect differences of opinion, however, and employed teachers who constantly questioned her decisions. Like Parkhurst, she was most definitely the head of the School. However, many former staff members who worked for both felt that Mrs. Durham was more accessible, that teachers could "go to her at any time and be heard with interest and respect." It is most probable, as one informant stated, that she was "more subtle about her management than Helen Parkhurst." Mrs. Durham's great personal warmth, her compassion displayed in dealing with individual staff members' problems, her advice given when it was needed, won the respect, if not always the love and admiration of her staff.

Charlotte Durham selected her board of trustees the same way she selected her staff. Technically, the board nominated prospective members from among the parent body. Mrs. Durham's influence was noted as being strongly influential, however, in the selection process. Her board was as diverse and interesting as her staff and very much concerned with educational policy.

There were some holdovers from Parkhurst's administration: some were interesting, well-known personalities, such as Orville Schell, William Shirer, Jacques Barzun, and Telford Taylor. Others included wealthy, concerned parents and a small cluster of Anglo-Saxon-like lawyers with impeccable educational credentials upon whom she came to depend and who were, in turn, devoted to her. These included Whitman Knapp, Stephen Duggan, and Richardson Wood. Educational questions were discussed, for example, the level at which students should begin French. A faculty representative, in this case, Mme. Frederic Ernst, would be invited before the board to state her opinion. A great issue during the fifties was the extent to which the school should provide psychological services. Teachers would be invited to present their curricula and board members participated in teacher-formed committees to evaluate educational goals. There seemed to be a great deal of communication between board members and staff in healthy collaborative effort towards making an already good school better.

While Charlotte Durham stressed the idea of a collaboration and surrounded herself with representatives from various constituent bodies such as the PTA and the Dalton Associates, she nevertheless constructed a regime based on personal loyalties that helped formulate and implement school policy. Again, this regime was, as far as I can ascertain, composed of her special group of board lawyers and her board treasurer; it also included such parent trustees as Elizabeth Steinway Chapin, a former Dalton graduate whose family was of great influence in the music world, and Marjorie Pleshette, who gave generously of her time as board secretary, and who initiated several fundraising projects, such as the thrift shop.

In 1944, ten years before the Supreme Court decision holding it unconstitutional for blacks to have to send their children to separate schools, Charlotte Durham became one of the first heads of an independent school to start a program of racial integration in the Lower School. Ten black children were accepted and placed among the three-, four-, and five-year old groups. The parents of these children were from such professions as medicine, law, dentistry, social work, and education. In addition, two black teaching assistants were hired, in order to help the black students gain confidence and assure their success. Many informants point to this event as "a big step" for the school, as it was feared that white parents would withdraw their children as a result of the program. In fact, very few did. In all, only four families directly affected by integration left Dalton that year; two explicitly stated that it was "because of Negroes."[6]

---

[6]Board of Trustees, Minutes, May 9, 1945.

Continuing in the spirit of integration and service to the community, an attempt to investigate the feasibility of securing Puerto Rican[7] children was initiated by longstanding trustee Helen Buttenwieser in February, 1958. Although no decisive action was taken at the time, the consciousness-raising process and the notion of the interrelatedness of school and society was still very much alive.

What of the characteristics of Dalton that gave it its particular flavor of individualism during the period of the founding of a variety of independent, progressive schools? What happened to House, Lab, Conference Assignments, Unit Cards, Progress Charts, Community Service? Was Charlotte Durham's statement valid that she never repudiated Helen Parkhurst's ideas but saw to it that they could function in an ordered way?

The Dalton Plan began in fifth grade. House, as a system of organizing and communicating with students, continued from the lower Middle School through the High School. It consisted of multi-age groups, meeting for a fixed period five times per week. A teacher, designated house advisor, presided. Student activities revolved around houses; student progress reports were administered by house advisors. House was considered so important a social unit that house reports (really citizenship reports) were written by house advisors and were sent to the college along with academic reports. There was much debate (and it still rages) as to the merits of a multi-age house. Many faculty members felt that it was an excellent way in which older and younger children could learn about each other developmentally, that it afforded an easy way of getting to know the Dalton community vertically, as well as horizontally. There were many faculty members, however, who felt that multi-age houses led to isolation by grade, since eighth graders would remain alone rather than mix with younger children freshmen would remain with freshmen rather than assimilate with upper classmen. Furthermore, although houses were small in number, usually sixteen members in the High School, four students from each class, the group dynamics must have been difficult to orchestrate.

Lab became a fixed block of time consisting of the first two periods

---

[7]Today there is disagreement about whether to use either the word Latino or the term Hispanic for people of Puerto Rican origin. It is not my intent to enter this debate here; rather, I am using the term that was used during this period.

in the daily schedule, five days per week. Lab commitments were written into the assignment. They were usually extensions of the assignments or remediation as in Dora Downes' famous "correct writing labs" in the High School, in which students would sit on kitchen chairs, often for hours, attempting to fathom what the red marks in the margin meant with respect to specific grammatical errors. Lab was conducted in the same room in which the teacher held conferences and usually involved groups of four or more students. Students would be responsible for organizing their groups and scheduling appointments on the teachers' calendars. Although the organization of lab was more flexible in the Middle School, the notion of student responsibility in the planning of time was present there, too. The faculty seems to have been concerned with students using lab effectively; the students seem to have been concerned with the availability of the faculty. These concerns are still present and continue to plague both faculty and students.

Conferences, called when a group of students reached the same point in the assignment, were now scheduled into the student's day, three times per week. In essence, the conference became the class. Class, a grade level academic meeting, ceased to exist.

Assignments, as a way of apportioning work to students in large blocks of time, usually four weeks, continued in many forms. Some were creative, suggesting projects and activities auxiliary to the curriculum, while others were mundane, listing required reading and page numbers. Apparently the shape of the assignment was determined by the individual teacher. Often it did not reflect the excitement and engagement of the student in a conference or lab.

Unit cards in the Middle School and progress charts in the High School functioned as ways in which house advisors could check on their advisees' progress. They also served as reminders to students of work yet to be done.

Student government continued both in the Middle and High Schools. Although it possessed little in the way of decision-making powers, it served as a learning experience in the democratic process. A government period was fixed in the schedule each week as were student committee meetings, revolving around the government. Thus, each student was expected to participate in government, if not in an open assembly, then through a committee.

Community service, a central idea in a school committed to

educating students who would be responsive to the needs of society, was expanded under the leadership of Nora Hodges, a language and social studies teacher. High school students, in the belief that "effective education for citizenship comes from direct association with the community,"[8] were placed one afternoon each week during their junior and senior years in hospitals, settlement houses, nursery schools, political campaign headquarters, and social service agencies such as Federation of Jewish Philanthropies and the Lighthouse for the Blind. They were visited in these sites by Mrs. Hodges and formally evaluated in their field work. Records of their performance were sent to colleges along with their academic grades.

The nursery, begun by Helen Parkhurst and continued by Charlotte Durham, continued to be a source of pride in the High School curriculum until a tragedy occurred in 1955–56. While under the joint care of a freshman and Miss Amott, a registered nurse in charge of the nursery, an infant died, apparently of an internal hemorrhage. Even though the nursery was shut down, Mrs. Durham supported its reopening.

A recurring concern that runs through board minutes and discussions with former teachers and students is Dalton's psychological services. Some felt that the services the school provided were unique at the time, that Dalton was very special in the way in which it treated the whole child. During Charlotte Durham's administration, Dr. Genevieve Coy taught a psychology course to seniors and worked with the faculty; Aysa Kadis and later her assistant, Janet Greene, worked with faculty, students, and parents. High School students were subjected to a yearly battery of psychological tests. Many recalled with glee drawing their houses, parents, and members of the opposite sex, or collaborating on ink blot slides to see such phenomena as rabbits in rhumba costumes. Levity aside, the breadth and scope of the services offered by the school seem unusually comprehensive. Each student, during his or her career at Dalton, was touched by it. Some conjecture that the composition of the student body demanded this; others, that the administration was sensitive to the psychological dimension of students' problems. More likely it was a combination of both factors.

A popular notion in progressive circles during the 1920s was that of "city and country." City children were brought to the country for lengthy blocks of time in order to acquaint them with the agrarian roots upon which

---

[8]Charlotte Durham, Board of Trustees Minutes, May 14, 1947.

their country was founded. Children would learn firsthand how butter was made, where eggs came from. They would see farm produce grown and come to understand how particular staples they took for granted came into being. Caroline Pratt, a contemporary of Helen Parkhurst, founded a school called "City and Country." Helen Parkhurst attempted to introduce the notion of "city and country" to Dalton through the New Milford Experiment and the Otis trip.

The New Milford Experiment was abandoned because of the cloudy financial arrangements Parkhurst had made concerning the property in New Milford. The Otis trip to George Dillman's farm in Otis, Massachusetts, continued to thrive and became an established third grade event. Dalton third graders twice a year visited Mr. Dillman's farm and learned not only about plants and domesticated farm animals, but also about living together in groups.

As I was studying the Durham administration, I was particularly impressed with the amount of "soul searching" done by faculty members, administrators, and board members. Faculty committees functioned throughout the 1940s in the areas of math, science, social studies, student records and reports, nursery and primary child study. Although I could not find documents from the years Dr. Ralph Tyler worked with the staff, I did find a wealth of material from 1953, when the staff and interested board members formed committees which met throughout the school year to examine the educational goals and life of the school.

The two most interesting surviving documents are those from the "Dead Wood Committee" and the "Serenity and the Development of the True Self Committee." The Dead Wood Committee dealt with such questions as the aims and purpose of education in general, problems of education arising from the demands of contemporary society, including the proper balance of freedom and guidance, the individual and his relation to the group. Questions about the Dalton Plan were posed, such as where might the Dalton Plan require "pruning or acceleration" to meet some of these general concerns. There were specific questions, such as: Should there be more creative arts? Why is so much remedial reading necessary? How much emphasis should be placed on preparing students to meet college entrance requirements? Should the balance between lab time and conference time be altered? Should house groupings and meetings be changed? Were traditional observances such as Book Day and Arch Day[9] still as meaningful to students as they were at their inception? These questions were hotly debated, and informants note that not all were resolved to the complete satisfaction of those involved.

The Serenity and the Development of the True Self committee was primarily concerned with the problem of "a consideration of how to maintain a balance between outer conditions and inner personal resources." Members of the committee voiced concern over pressures students encountered from school, parents, and peer groups. It was noted that the Dalton Plan "was created largely to avoid pressures upon children, because of unscheduled time called laboratory time."[10] The attitude of teachers was thought to create pressure because "teachers are apt to be too anxious to teach, rather than to let children learn."[11] The group concluded, somewhat naively, that if teachers were taught to use the Dalton Plan and students were taught to budget their time the problem of pressure could disappear. It is interesting to note in passing that the questions and concerns raised by both committees are still debated, perhaps in part reflecting the demands of society upon the school. Perhaps the particular problems arise because of the process-oriented nature of the Dalton Plan.

The questions still remain for the educational historian tracing the development of an independent progressive school from its early days through the sixties: What was Dalton really like in the forties and fifties? What factors were responsible for its change from a helter-skelter, crisis-oriented school to an organized, established educative institution?

Visitors to Dalton during Charlotte Durham's administration would have been hard pressed to label the school "progressive" or "traditional." The vocabulary of Helen Parkhurst remained, but the school had settled into a routinized way of life, a pattern, institutional historian David Rothman

---

[9]Book Day was celebrated on Lincoln's birthday. Each student was expected to donate a book to the school library. Arch Day was an end of the year ritual. Each student walked through a flowered covered arch on stage to signify his/her passage into the next grade. Helen Parkhurst instituted this practice, supposedly based on a Chinese custom.

[10]Minutes of the Serenity and Development of the True Self Committee (New York: Dalton School Archives, 1953), n.p.

[11]Ibid.

notes, common to the internal dynamics of many institutions. Additionally, there were many formal, if downright genteel characteristics, to Dalton not unlike those found in more established independent schools, such as Chapin, Spence, and Brearley. High school students would be expected to rise when adults entered the classroom; they wore smocks over their clothes, uniforms, if you will, the conditions of which were carefully supervised by a tyrannical yet genteel lady named Margaret who held sway over the coat room. Teachers were addressed by their full names, and it was not an unknown phenomenon for students appearing in school with too much makeup to be sent home. This was hardly the atmosphere of New Lincoln or Walden, "pure progressive schools," in the eyes of Daltonians, where students could wear blue jeans and address teachers by their first names.

However, there was much to make Dalton as "different" if not overly "progressive" to visitors. Children appeared to be unsupervised in the lower grades as well as the upper grades; there were many different activities taking place within one classroom; conferences, in the High School were held in semi-circles on kitchen-like chairs, and in many instances the teacher became part of the semi-circle.

The direction of an independent school is determined by a multitude of factors. Through my research and experience with independent schools, I have come to believe that for Dalton one of the most important factors governing the direction of the school is its head.

Charlotte Durham was an articulate, educated, genteel woman. Her presence in the school was ubiquitous. Three days per week she would walk through its corridors, stopping to talk with students, visiting classes. She knew each student's name on sight. Her educational philosophy was based on a genuine concern for the child. She saw the school as providing an environment in which "egocentric individuals can be transformed into socially responsible and socially energized people."[12] Ideally, with a Dalton education students would be able to think clearly and independently, "make judgements and discriminate among values," have acquired "sound work habits, proper skills and tools with which to carry out ideas," be "responsible human beings and citizens."[13] Hardly revolutionary ideas in 1947. Did not educational reformers such as Horace Mann and Henry

---

[12]Board of Trustees Minutes, May 14, 1947.
[13]Ibid.

Barnard a hundred years earlier voice similar sentiments?

Charlotte Durham's unique contribution to Dalton was to legitimize the school in the eyes of other independent guild schools. Under her leadership Dalton became a member of the Guild of Independent Schools; meetings were held at Dalton; eventually Mrs. Durham became the Guild head. She also attended meetings of independent boarding school associations, established contacts with colleges and instituted an experimental student teaching program with Barnard College. Significantly, discussions of Dalton as an "experimental school" were dropped in board minutes by the late forties.

Her task was a difficult one, indeed, during an era when Dalton had a large Jewish enrollment, and other independent Guild schools had little or none; when Dalton had in its employ Priscilla Hiss, wife of Alger Hiss, during a time when the mood of the establishment in New York City was decidedly against Hiss so much so that Priscilla Hiss often required a police escort from school.

It was, however, mandatory that Dalton change and adopt the characteristics of its "sister schools" if it was to survive. One important factor was that the clientele demanded it. Parents who sent their children to Dalton consisted of three types: those genuinely interested in progressive education, those whose children could not succeed in traditional schools, and those who lived in the neighborhood and chose Dalton because it was convenient or because they were excluded from other independent schools for religious reasons. In the "neighborhood group" fell many Protestant families who often left Dalton for formal and socially acceptable schools after the primary grades. As for the Jewish population, there were few schools open to them which would provide academic excellence, formal tone, and neighborhood accessibility. Because this neighborhood group formed the largest segment of the Dalton population, they became a powerful force in influencing the direction of the school.

Another important factor in Dalton's more "traditional" orientation was concern over college admissions. Because the colleges now required knowledge in specific areas, because graduating students became increasingly college bound until the 1950s, when virtually all members of the senior classes went off to college, the curriculum became academically oriented and followed a sequential, chronological progression in English and social studies, skill building in math, sciences, and languages. In the High School, students were required to take four years of English and social studies, three years of science, three years of math, four years of one language or a combination of three years of one and two of another. There was little choice involved on the part of the student as to what courses to elect.

The mood of the country had changed. The Truman and Eisenhower administrations, and in particular the McCarthy hearings, had encouraged a wave of conservatism in politics and conformity in living styles. At the same time, progressive education found itself under attack. In 1949, Bernard Iddings Bell's book, *Crisis in Education*, appeared. In 1953, Arthur E. Bestor's book, *Education Wastelands*, voiced even more articulate, logical, persuasive arguments against progressive education. Then Sputnik in 1957, helped to eclipse further the ideas of the progressives who saw the school as a lever of social reform. The schools, according to the new wave of critics, were to become places in which to mass produce scientists who would make the United States "number one" again. This would be done by going "back to basics," "squeezing the water out of the curriculum," as Bestor recommended, attending to and rewarding academic excellence.

In 1959, significantly the same year that H.G. Rickover published *Education and Freedom*, Charlotte Durham announced her plans to retire within the year. A search committee for a new head was established and Elizabeth Evarts, former head of the Lower School, was named acting head for the following school year. Some informants state that Mrs. Evarts was Charlotte Durham's choice for successor but that the board felt her vision too limited to meet the needs of the school in the sixties. She served as acting headmistress from 1960 to 1961. During her tenure the board selected Jack Kittell to succeed Charlotte Durham.

Charlotte Durham served Dalton as headmistress for eighteen years. She reunited a faculty torn by factionalism, revitalized a financially floundering institution, introduced racial integration, continued the Dalton Plan, and routinized and gave the school an air of respectability. All the while she managed to cater to a diverse clientele and retain the special flavor of the school: a healthy balance between academic excellence and artistic endeavor, between freedom of the individual and responsibility to the community.

5

THE KITTELL INTERLUDE (1961-1964)

Jack Edward Kittell was headmaster of Dalton from 1961 to 1964. During these four years, plans were formulated for the future direction of the Dalton School.

Jack Kittell was the third head of Dalton and the first man in the key leadership position. He succeeded a woman who had been its headmistress for eighteen years. Charlotte Durham, his predecessor, had been born and educated in the East; her expertise was in English literature, her experience in the independent schools. Kittell, although born in Rochester, New York, grew up in Coffeeville, Kansas. While still in high school, he decided that he would like to teach history; he concentrated in the social sciences at Coffeeville (Junior) College, majoring in psychology.[1] Kittell completed his undergraduate work at the University of Denver; the outbreak of World War II interrupted his plan for graduate study. He joined the G-5 program at Vanderbilt University and received instruction in languages and "areas in Western Europe for civilian governments."[2]

After the war, Jack Kittell moved to the state of Washington where his wife's family was located. He completed a master's degree at Central Washington College of Education. His teaching experience included five years in Union Gap, Washington at a special school that functioned as a bridge to the high schools in Yakima.[3] It was designed to serve both the children of the rural community of Union Gap and children of migratory farm workers. During his first year there, an experimental "outdoor school" was instituted so that an outdoor experience became an integral part of the

---

[1] *The Dalton Bulletin* (New York: Dalton School Archives, December 1960), p. 3.
[2] Ibid.
[3] Ibid., p. 4.

curriculum, thus facilitating the integration of an itinerant group of students into the community, as well as acquainting them with the rudiments of seventh and eighth grade studies. Kittell states that it was his Union Gap experience that stimulated his interest in the "total educational experience."[4]

From Union Gap, Jack Kittell moved on to Washington State College[5] where he obtained his doctorate in education. Four years before he assumed the position of headmaster of Dalton, he was affiliated with the University of California at Berkeley. While at Berkeley, Kittell served as Assistant Professor of Education, Coordinator of Elementary Laboratory Schools, Advisor to Graduates, and Director of the University's Summer Demonstration Elementary School.

The Kittell years at Dalton almost parallel the Kennedy years at the White House. During this time, many college students throughout the nation were eagerly reading Ian Fleming thrillers and fantasizing about a career in the C.I.A. Others, more idealistically inclined, enrolled in the Peace Corps, believing in the immortal words of John F. Kennedy: "Ask not what your country can do for you but, rather, ask what you can do for your country." There was a general feeling of optimism and idealism among young people.

At the same time, critics of progressive education, such as Arthur Bestor, were crying for "back to basics" in the schools. In 1959 at Woods Hole, Massachusetts, thirty-five scholars assembled to consider ways in which to improve elementary and secondary science school teaching. "University science professors dominated the conference, whose chairman was Harvard psychologist Jerome S. Bruner."[6] A month after the conference, James B. Conant's *The American High School Today* was published. Conant advocated retaining the comprehensive high school, arguing that small schools did not meet the needs of nor challenge students functioning in today's world. He also supported ability grouping and special testing to identify the gifted in order to provide them with advanced placement. Jerome S. Bruner's book, *The Process of Education*, followed shortly behind Conant's.

---

[4]Ibid., p. 5.

[5]Which later became Washington State University.

[6]Franklin Parker, "Ideas that Shaped American High Schools," *Phi Delta Kappan*, January, 1981, pp. 314–19.

The Process of Education, Bruner's report on the Woods Hole conference, contained a philosophical and psychological justification for using the "discovery" or "inquiry" method of learning with the gifted. The book's message, "Any subject can be taught effectively in some intellectually honest form to any child at any stage of development,"[7] deeply affected the thinking of both Jack Kittell and his successor, Donald Barr.

When Jack Kittell became headmaster, he inherited an interesting but a static and staid school. Once in the foreground of educational experimentalism, Dalton had become a stabilized, well-known, educationally sound institution. It would require a strong, creative, forceful leader to bring about changes necessary to meet the needs of a post-Sputnik society. Additionally, Dalton's faculty and Board of Trustees were a sophisticated group of people, exercising an unusual amount of autonomy during the interim period between Mrs. Durham's resignation and Dr. Kittell's appointment.

Dr. Kittell was very much aware of what was happening in educational circles. One informant, a former trustee, vividly remembers Kittell giving her a copy of Bruner's book to read. There is also an important document compiled by Kittell regarding the future direction of Dalton, echoing the Conant report. Kittell's problem, however, was not lack of intellectual ability, but rather a lack of Eastern ways. His inability to relate to Eastern cultural patterns was mentioned by many informants; his public style, characterized by one informant as "clutzy," attempting to be humorous and instead falling on his face in large gatherings, alienated both faculty members and parents. Additionally, he was "tainted by his public school background" and accused by one informant of possessing "a School Superintendent's mentality." He was a gentleman but an uninspiring one, "a good man practically broken in the process" of heading a school in transition. Donald Barr characterized Jack Kittell as "the unsung hero of Dalton"[8] as well might he be. Unfortunately, he failed to muster the support necessary to create a regime that would have helped him implement the changes he was entrusted to make.

Although informants speak of Dr. Kittell as being ineffectual and point to the fact that during his long illness the faculty and trustees ran the

---

[7]Ibid., p. 318.

[8]Charles Fisher's taped interview with Donald Barr, October 14, 1980.

school, the divisional directors reporting directly to the president of the board, he did compile a document combining the ideas of the Goals Committee of the board, faculty recommendations and educational ideas then in vogue indicating the future direction the school would take.[9] How much of this document is actually the work of Dr. Kittell is impossible to determine; a particularly knowledgeable informant attributes most of the ideas to the board president, Alfred Stern. In any event, Dr. Kittell presented a document to the board, included in the minutes of June, 1962, stating four goals in the development of Dalton's future:

1. Quality through diversity
2. Expansion
3. The addition of boys in the High School
4. The addition of thirteenth and fourteenth grades.[10]

The ideas of quality through diversity, expansion, and inclusion of boys in the High School speak for themselves. The addition of thirteenth and fourteenth grades was thought to service the "late bloomer" population, not quite ready for college. Interestingly enough, this latter proposal was the only one not implemented during the next administration.

Although Dr. Kittell did not remain at Dalton to see the first three goals become a reality, a massive fundraising drive was begun during his tenure under trustee Harris Huey; a parent, James Dinerman, was called in to help decide the optimum number of students for Dalton, and an investigation was begun to decide whether or not to add on to the existing building at 89th Street or to purchase another building.

Not everyone was in favor of the new direction the school was planning to take. There was a group on the board against expansion and coeducation in the High School; many parents and alumni also objected to a "larger" coeducational Dalton. Nevertheless, the "powerbrokers," a small group of committed, visionary trustees, were determined to make Dalton into the best school in the city.

---

[9]This document was probably an abbreviated version of an earlier one prepared in March, 1962, at the request of the Board of Trustees.

[10]The total document was originally included in the Board Of Trustees Minutes of June 1962.

The board minutes from Dr. Kittell's administration are filled with reports of fundraising proposals, such as a thrift shop, an art show and budget concerns. However, the school continued to function, carrying forth the ideas of the Dalton Plan, modifying, enriching the learning experience for its students.

The High School, run by Rebecca Straus, became involved in a Puerto Rican student exchange; five high school Spanish-speaking students went to Puerto Rico for over two weeks and then hosted back their Puerto Rican counterparts. Experimenting in scheduling took place; conferences would meet as one large group once a week; then two smaller groups would each meet additionally, twice more. New courses were added in the High School, such as History of Drama, Plane Geometry in grade nine, indicating a concern for presenting a richer, more challenging and diverse curriculum.

In the upper Middle School, under the direction of Michael Casey, reforms were undertaken to enable "capable children to move more rapidly and more intensively through the major curriculum."[11] Basically, the reforms included more formalized conferences, more structured lab time, and a longer school day. French and Spanish were introduced in the fifth grade; corrective English classes in grades four through eight.

In the Primary Division, under Eileen Clarke, the cuisiniere method was introduced in mathematics; cursive handwriting was taught in third grade. The nursery was eliminated because it was too expensive and the school needed the space for additional classrooms. In its place, Dalton decided to sponsor a day nursery at the Benjamin Franklin Housing Project at 100th Street and Second Avenue. It was hoped that high school students would elect to work with infants and young children for community service.

Dr. Kittell's own imprint could be found in two areas: raising faculty salaries and utilizing the plant on weekends. When Dr. Kittell came to Dalton, he was appalled by the salaries paid to the teachers. He fought for raises and for additional staff members. Although he was successful in both areas, his victory was pyrrhic—for he lost the support of the board president in the process.

In 1961, Dr. Kittell began discussing a Saturday program in order to fully utilize the school plant. It was not adopted until 1962, and, to the surprise of the board, a Saturday group for middle school boys was popular

---

[11]Board of Trustees Minutes, "Letter to Parents," January 21, 1963.

among the parents and actually made money. Summer programs as well were under consideration. In particular, Dr. Kittell suggested to the board at a meeting in December 1962, that a six week summer session be held at Dalton for high school students. A course in statistics would be taught by math teacher Stuart Hanlon; a course in chemistry would be offered as well as arts and swimming programs. Dr. Kittell was given the board's permission to investigate the proposal further. Although this, too, was not implemented during Dr. Kittell's tenure, it served as the basis for Dalton's summer school and Dalton's summer day camp implemented during the Barr administration.

In 1964, Jack Kittell resigned from his position. His resignation was accepted by then board president, Alfred R. Stern. Kittell's health had not been good; he was a Westerner at heart, and he wished to return to California with his family. His legacy to Dalton was his blueprint for the future.

6

THE BARR YEARS (1964–1974)

When Donald Barr became Headmaster of Dalton in 1964, he found a school on the verge of a transformation from a small, Upper East Side, independent, progressive school with a single sex high school division to a large, fully coeducational, comprehensive school. His predecessor, Jack Kittell, had, on request from the trustees, formulated the plans for Dalton's future. It remained the task of Donald Barr to implement them.

He succeeded. In a scant ten years, the school more than doubled its population, opened the pre-kindergarten through first grade division at 61 East 91st Street, rebuilt the gymnasium and expanded library facilities at 89th Street, extended coeducation through the High School, and acquired an additional gymnasium at 215 East 94th Street.

So much for measurable results. Donald Barr did something far more important for Dalton than build buildings and, of course, help raise the money for them. He took over a mildly interesting school, going nowhere, and made it desirable, a "hot school," so to speak. Donald Barr gave Dalton "pizazz."

He did so amidst one of the most difficult decades in contemporary history: the sixties. This decade, which we are just beginning to sort out, had certain undeniable benchmarks: Vietnam, the Kennedy and King assassinations, Bob Dylan and the Beatles, psychedelia and drugs, Watts, S.D.S., the Black Panthers, and N.O.W., not to mention the sexual revolution, beginning in the twenties, coming to fruition in the sixties.

It was the rapidity with which events occurred that was so unnerving. When Lyndon Johnson gave his "Great Society" speech at the University of Michigan in May, 1964, little did anyone think that scarcely two years later disillusionment would set in. Yet in July, 1966, black ghettos burned in Cleveland and Chicago, civil rights workers were beaten and shot at in the South, and casualty lists mounted in Vietnam.

Few who lived through the sixties would claim to be untouched by this decade in which the Great Society appeared to be "coming apart." It was against this backdrop that Donald Barr attempted to inject his commitment to academic rigor and his philosophy of conservatism into the Dalton community.

Who was Donald Barr? Donald Barr was born in New York City
in 1921. He was educated at the Lincoln School, exemplary of the best of
progressive education in New York City, and graduated from Columbia
College in 1941, having majored in two fields: mathematics and anthropology. He served in the Army in 1943, "taught math and Italian,"[1] "never saw
action,"[2] and returned to graduate school. He married in 1946, taught
English to undergraduates at Columbia for ten years and was Assistant Dean
of the Engineering School for seven years. In 1963, he became an Associate
Program Director for the National Science Foundation in Washington, D.C.
Barr has three sons, all of whom attended an independent school in New
York. Additionally, he was active in local Morningside Heights politics,
wrote articles, reviewed books.

During his tenure as Headmaster, he authored three books:
Arithmetic for Billy Goats, explaining the "new Math," *Who Pushed Humpty
Dumpty*, a collection of his ideas about education, and *Strangers in a
Strange Land*, a science fiction book heavily infused with sex.

Donald Barr, like Helen Parkhurst, still evokes strong emotions;
informants describing Barr used strongly polarized words such as "genius"
or "madman" in attempting to characterize Dalton's former Headmaster. An
accurate, and fair portrait of him, I believe, is as follows:

> ...an intellectual, a Renaissance man. He is brilliant, well-
> read, formidably articulate, at home in science and math as
> well as in English and the arts. He can also be rigid, and
> at times conversations can turn into monologues. He does
> not ask people their opinions or questions about them-
> selves. Yet...[he] has an uncanny, intuitive ability to
> encapsulate incisively and instantly a student's or a teach-
> er's personality. And he is capable of acts of real kindness
> and compassion, particularly when an emergency arises.[3]

---

[1] Donald Barr as quoted in *The New York Post*, October 17, 1973, p. 47.
[2] Ibid.
[3] Peter Gibbon, "Hartwick: Portrait of an Independent School" (Ph.D.
dissertation, Teachers College, Columbia University, 1980).

Whatever one's personal feelings towards Donald Barr, he cannot be accused of not having definite ideas about education. He was well aware of many current school problems, such as "de-intellectualized curriculum, the failure to educate in serious subjects, the neglect of academically gifted children."[4] He supported a rigorous course of study, one that would allow for a rich and varied curriculum. He permitted high school students the freedom of choosing their own courses through introduction of a serious elective program, accelerated able students, provided seminars and tutorials, often run by professionals in their fields, as in the case of photographer Ken Hyman or advertising consultant Tony Schwartz. In 1962, Dalton offered French, Spanish, and Latin to high school students. In 1970, Dalton offered Latin, Greek, Hebrew, Chinese, French, German, Italian, Japanese, Russian and Spanish.

"The curriculum at Dalton is—as it is intended to be—somewhat demanding."[5] Under the Barr administration, students in the primary grades (N–3), now called the First Program, began reading instruction whenever they showed interest in reading. Students in the Middle School studied literature along with grammar and spelling; students in the High School would choose their electives as if in college, although within the four years each student would be required to take a one-semester course in composition, poetry, novel and drama. Languages were begun in the Middle School; science was introduced in the First Program and taught at all levels by specialist teachers from the department. In addition to biological and physical sciences, behavioral sciences such as psychology and anthropology were offered both in the Middle and High School. Social studies began in the First Program and continued through the High School, the last two years consisting of elective courses. There were two sequences, chronologically presented, introduced in the first and last years of middle school, consisting of world history, including American and Asian history. Math began with "simple counting in the earliest years of school" and continued throughout the divisions. Students could elect math courses to suit their achievement level; thus certain students might study calculus in grade nine, others in

---

[4]Richard Hofstadter, *Anti-intellectualism in American Life* (New York: Vintage Books, 1962), p. 103.

[5]*The Dalton School* (New York: Dalton Archives, 1970–71), p. 12 (pamphlet).

grade eleven.

> Dalton places unusual emphasis on the arts and offers a
> variety of courses and extracurricular "activities" in
> painting, sculpture, graphics, motion-picture and still
> photography, printing, woodworking and other crafts,
> acting, stage design and construction, vocal and instrumen-
> tal music, modern dance, musical composition, the history
> of art, and the history of music. The studio arts, some of
> the crafts, and instrumental music begin in the First
> Program; the rest, including musical composition, begin in
> Middle School.[6]

This unusual emphasis on the arts, a tradition established by Helen
Parkhurst and further encouraged by Charlotte Durham, flourished during
Barr's administration. Students could concentrate in the arts, visual or
performing, for credit, or they could elect "interest" areas for nonacademic
credit. The offerings were impressive: in the Visual Arts category, twenty-
three courses were listed, ranging from "Painting I" to "Costume Design
and Construction."

The physical education program was equally impressive, for it not
only accommodated students in the High School, it allowed the nonathlete
a number of choices to learn sports in a noncompetitive setting. Thus, there
were team sports and interest sports; among the latter were judo, fencing,
gymnastics, tennis. This program, allowing Dalton students to participate in
intermural sports but at the same time accommodating those individuals not
electing to play on teams or, in some cases, the nonathlete, was worked
through by the Educational Policies Committee of the Board of Trustees
under the leadership of Professor Lawrence A. Cremin. This committee was
also influential in recommending the expansion of Dalton's physical
education facilities, leading to the creation of a new gymnasium at the 89th
Street building and the purchase of another building at 215 East 94th Street
to be used by the physical education and dance departments.

For those students with "special interest," tutorials were available.
These tutorials were accessible to high school students and some middle

---

[6]Ibid., p. 13.

school students. Seniors were encouraged to pursue Senior Projects. With faculty sponsorship, a senior classman could choose to write the equivalent of a master's essay on the subject of his/her choice, produce and direct a play, compose and perform a work of music. Thus, the curriculum allowed for student interest; it also provided high school students and some middle school students a measure of autonomy in choosing their individual courses of study; additionally, it provided for individual differences as talented students could move ahead rapidly while others could elect courses which would accommodate their achievement level.

For an interesting and varied curriculum to work, it must be introduced by an interesting and varied instructional staff. Donald Barr, in the tradition of Helen Parkhurst and Charlotte Durham, selected a group of interesting people, proficient in their subject matter. A French aristocrat taught American and European history, a Hungarian countess taught Russian and French, while an aristocratic Yugoslavian, raised in France, taught French and Russian. The High School was headed by a descendent of an aristocratic White Russian family. A phenomenon of the time was the availability of a group of young men, recent college graduates, who chose to teach before entering professional schools rather than flee to Canada or fight in Vietnam. Particularly under Barr, a degree from a school of education was considered a deficit to prospective teachers seeking employment at Dalton, save in the First Program.

In both the determination of curriculum and selection of staff, Barr played an active role:

> I once called the English chairman in and simply announced that the high-school English program would no longer consist of a Freshman English course, followed by a Sophomore English course, etc., but would consist of about twenty well-defined electives—Major British Novels, The Epic, The Theater of Social Protest, Humor and Satire, Modern British and American Poetry, Short Story Writing, The Craft of Poetry, that sort of thing—from which each student might choose with only a very general distributive requirement and a very few restrictions on eligibility to constrain him. I suppose there was a depart-

mental discussion about it; I do not remember going.[7]

A similar event occurred in the Social Studies Department. Barr arrived at a meeting, and by "ukase," announced that American history would be taught in grades four, seven, and ten. All prospective staff members underwent an interview with Donald Barr, as well as with the appropriate divisional director.

Barr's educational philosophy also included the banning of objective tests from Dalton High School classrooms. Teachers were given to understand that the only valid form of testing was the essay, for it allowed students to share with them their thought processes by which they arrived at their answers. Donald Barr also took on the College Examination Board in his book *Who Pushed Humpty Dumpty?*

It is difficult to argue with Barr's logic and eloquence, especially when he states that if objective tests are to be given, the child should be allowed to review his answer sheet with the examiner, for "It is not in a child's command of facts or skills, but in his wonderful errors, that we often catch the first shocking glimpse of his talent."[8] The problem for many classroom teachers was that students did not have adequate preparation in taking objective tests, so that when they faced the CEEB tests—tests which in part determined which college they might attend—their performances were not as good as they might have been with more practice in this area.

In holding with his disdain for standardized tests, Donald Barr reviewed the admissions process in the school with the help of the Educational Policies Committee and had the school psychologist and appropriate divisional directors devise special tests for prospective Dalton students. The ERB tests, universally considered "valid" by New York's independent schools, were no longer adequate determinants for future Daltonians. In point of fact, this policy led to much speculation among prospective parents as to just what the school was looking for in their students. Barr, however, clarified this somewhat in the *New York Times Magazine* article on Dalton when he stated that Dalton students have "pizazz." And Dalton students, quick to follow through, appeared shortly

---

[7]Donald Barr, *Who Pushed Humpty Dumpty?* (New York: Atheneum, 1971), p. 123.
[8]Ibid., p. 160.

thereafter sporting "pizazz" buttons on their clothing.

Having banned objective testing as much as possible, Barr also took a firm stance against "canned curriculum." Teachers were encouraged to devise their own materials. They were discouraged from attending professional workshops and book exhibits weighted towards educational matter. Again, Barr's thinking in this area is fully expressed in his book *Who Pushed Humpty Dumpty?*

Donald Barr and his staff made Dalton an exciting place in which students could learn. Subjects were departmentalized; departments were vertically organized, often cutting across divisions; instruction was individualized, whenever possible. Staff was shared in all disciplines in the Middle and High Schools. This gave faculty the opportunity to work with students at many different developmental levels. It also provided additional enrichment for students as they had exposure to faculty with particular areas of expertise at earlier levels.

"House" and "Lab" continued as integral parts of the Dalton Plan, House now specifically concerned with "the social life and personal development" of students; Lab as concerned with "quasi-tutorial problems and project sessions." Lab rooms for the disciplines were created, allowing students and teachers easy access to one another. Assignments were given to students again, in large blocks usually four weeks in duration, and were considered the students' contracts which they could modify with their teachers to suit "interests, aptitudes or problems." Progress charts and unit cards gradually fell by the wayside as school size increased and boys were admitted to the High School.

The Dalton Plan officially still began in sixth grade, although teachers at various grade levels could choose to introduce parts of it which they judged appropriate to the age level of their students.

During this time, the student body increased from about 560 to over 1,200. As the school began to increase its enrollment and admit boys into the High School, its fundraising activities swung into high gear. A drive was established, "The Dalton Fund," spearheaded by trustees Harry Huey and Alfred Stern and the auxiliary services such as the PTA, the Alumni Association and the floundering Dalton Associates were encouraged to develop plans for benefits and other activities which would raise money.

The PTA responded accordingly, taking over the traditional Middle School Spring Fair and turning it into a semi-professional Spring Fair and celebrity studded auction to benefit the school. Dalton, through this endeavor, received much publicity, both positive and negative. Additionally, the PTA with Dalton Associates also started a thrift shop which became a surprisingly profitable operation.

Summer programs were started for preschoolers through high school. The Dalton Day Camp and the Dalton Summer School brought in revenue during the summer months and allowed maximum utilization of the physical plants throughout the year.

An interesting experiment, too, was attempted by trustee Lawrence Buttenwieser, in accordance with Dalton's traditional commitment to integration. In May, 1968, he announced at a board meeting that the school was searching for fifteen black and Puerto Rican children "whose need is total" from a single geographic area around East 104th Street. Furthermore, he stated that entrants would be in grades one through four; contributions of $2,500 per year for twelve years would be sought for each child, and that there were six applicants ready for acceptance. To help children with adjustment problems, a part-time psychological social worker would be added to the staff. What was innovative in this plan was the concept of taking a group of children, from a particular geographic area, requiring full financial assistance, thus allowing for support within the group after school hours.

The plan in concept was a good one; its success rate was somewhat disappointing; it did ultimately provide additional support services to Dalton students. Few of the children from this group finished high school; the number I found was three. The rest of the group dropped out in the middle school years for a variety of reasons. The black children had difficulty communicating with the social worker who was Puerto Rican; many of the children came from families not committed to the school's particular philosophy, and thus they may not have received appropriate support from the home.[9] Additionally, some of these children were verbally disadvan-

---

[9]Research suggests that the philosophy and pedagogic practices at schools such as Dalton reflect the particular class interests of the upper middle classes who send their children to these schools. For example, Basil Bernstein's work on invisible pedagogy, similar to Dalton's pedagogic practices, argues that such pedagogy is social class rooted. See Basil Bernstein, *Class, Codes and Control, Volume 3* (London: Routledge, 1975) and *The Structuring of Pedagogic Discourse, Class, Codes and Control,*

taged compared to their Dalton counterparts in the use of standard English and middle class communication codes,[10] and quick to use physical actions rather than words when in conflict with their advantaged peers. In one incident, a frustrated and angry black student bit a teacher. Under Lawrence A. Cremin's direction, the Education Policies Committee of the Board of Trustees in November, 1968, recognized the obvious tensions, especially those of "acculturation and radical change in the environment" of these students. It was hoped that their problems could be solved by the guidance counselors and the classroom teachers involved. Unfortunately, this did not happen.

Dalton did gain from this experiment. Three specialists in learning disorders and emotional problems were added to the staff for students requiring additional academic support in order to meet with success in school. Teachers were also helped in acquiring strategies for students with learning problems. The Preceptoral Department began, in part, as a support system for this particular group of children, became a place where all students could come for help and encouragement.

Thus Dalton, as it is today, took shape during the Barr administration. The plan that Jack Kittell had formulated became a reality under Barr.

Volume 4 (London: Routledge, 1990). See also, Alan R. Sadovnik, "Basil Bernstein's Theory of Pedagogic Practice: A Structuralist Approach," *Sociology of Education*, January 1991, pp. 48–63. For a historical discussion of the relationship between Bernstein's work and schools such as Dalton see Susan F. Semel, "Bernstein and the History of American Education," forthcoming in Alan R. Sadovnik, *Basil Bernstein: Consensus and Controversy* (Norwood, N.J.: Ablex Publishing Corporation, forthcoming). Additionally, recent studies indicate that families from lower socio-economic backgrounds are disadvantaged in terms of parental involvement due to differences in cultural capital. See, for example, Annette Lareau, *Home Advantage* (London: Falmer Press, 1989).

[10] For a discussion of social class and sociolinguistic codes, see Basil Bernstein, *Class, Codes and Control, Volume 1* (London: Routledge, 1973). For a discussion of the controversy surrounding Bernstein's theory of class differences in communication codes see Basil Bernstein, *The Structuring of Pedagogic Discourse*, and Alan R. Sadovnik, *Basil Bernstein: Consensus and Controversy*.

Success is measurable here by simply looking at the rich curriculum, interesting and talented student body and staff, impressive physical plant, financial stability, and college admissions. Yet Dalton, under Donald Barr, was rife with controversy which erupted in what could be termed the "Great Schism," in 1970. Furthermore, four years later, the Headmaster resigned without warning.

There were a number of underlying causes for the unrest and tension during the Barr years. The first, as was mentioned earlier, was the decade itself. The second was the rapid increase in school size and the accompanying dislocation. Almost every informant discussed school size as a problem. Additionally, a report prepared by E. Belvin Williams for the Education Policies Committee of the Board of Trustees, on December 2, 1971, focused on this issue. Statements such as "a sense of smallness, camaraderie and intimacy has been lost," "it feels too big," and "it seems crowded," appear. However, Mr. Williams countered these statements with the opposing view that school mirrors the real world—"e.g., reduced space." Whatever the case, people who experienced Dalton before it became a large school or during the process of its expansion had adjustment problems. Old Dalton families, very clannish, complained about being pushed out of the auxiliary services by the new people who brought money or fundraising expertise to the school or both. Students complained that they did not know their classmates' names or that they could not find seats in the lunchroom. Teachers complained that they no longer had classrooms but shared space, and were reduced to the status of traveling salesmen peddling their wares from classroom to classroom. Parents complained about the way high school students in various stages of undress leaned on the parked cars in front of the school building. The size of the High School enrollment alone was the same size as the entire school enrollment during Kittell's administration. Theft and vandalism increased.

A third factor in the general unrest was the style of this particular headmaster. Of all the heads of Dalton, Donald Barr most resembles its founder, Helen Parkhurst. Both had definite educational philosophies; both had a sense of style—or flamboyance; both loved publicity; and both could talk the most impecunious parents into dipping into their bank account to give a few dollars to Dalton. But "Parkie" was ubiquitous; Barr was not.

Helen Parkhurst administered Dalton almost tyrannically, often at random. But she was forgiven her faults because she was the founder of the school. Not until money problems became overwhelming did the trustees take matters into their own hands. Donald Barr, in style, was much like Parkhurst. He administered the school, in his own words, "by ukase"; he had little apparent rational organization; the crisis-solution method was the most popular way of solving problems. For many years, it worked.

Donald Barr relied upon a number of people from the board, staff, and parent body to help him formulate and implement school policy. His support on the board came from such members as James Dinerman, who served as treasurer, Arthur Richenthal, a prominent New York lawyer who served as president, and, initially, Gordon Smith, who succeeded James Dinerman as treasurer. Barr's support on his administrative staff came from Durham holdover Georgia C. Rice, who carefully screened all of Barr's appointments, ran the school in his absence, and supervised financial matters; and from Middle School director Michael Casey. Barr also met regularly, often after hours, with several staff members: science teacher Margot Gumport, English teacher Hortense Tyroler, school psychologist Janet Greene, and librarian Mary Alexander. Margot Gumport was a Dalton graduate married to a successful New York surgeon. Hortense Tyroler was a venerable member of the faculty from the days of Charlotte Durham whose influence was felt in the German Jewish community through her husband's connections. Janet Greene had access to Dalton families through her private practice, and Mary Alexander was a close friend of Georgia C. Rice. Each of these women had longevity and access to students, parents, and faculty. Each provided Donald Barr with broad-based information and helped disseminate the administration's point of view in the faculty dining room and at New York dinner parties and social clubs where Dalton families were present. Barr's support among the parent body came from "new admit" families such as the David Evinses, the Morton Janklows, the Arnold Ginsburgs, and the Henry Epsteins. These families initiated fundraising activities and supported Barr during the attempt to unseat him in 1970.

Donald Barr assumed the responsibility for decision-making, arguing, "On my head be it."[11] He held his teachers in disdain, frequently criticizing them at public gatherings. He tolerated bizarre behavior in students who normally would have been expelled; he did not uniformly enforce school regulations.

And he loved to talk. At faculty meetings, parent meetings; on

---

[11]Ibid., p. 124.

radio, television and in newspapers, magazines, from *The New York Times* to *Penthouse*, Donald Barr willingly gave his opinion on any topic that arose. He was urbane, witty, entertaining—"the give 'em Hell Headmaster." One informant present at fundraising cocktail parties stated that listening to Barr was like watching the Tonight Show, with Johnny Carson, nightly.

Barr held court in his office, often in his shirt sleeves, prominently displaying his omnipresent red suspenders. The second floor, once a quiet, dignified sanctuary under Charlotte Durham, became the hub of Dalton's universe, with the High School Director's office a stone's throw from the Headmaster's. Parents in the lobby and on the second floor became a familiar sight.

> In its sustained and often frantic search for a new freedom, American youth in the 60s turned to drugs in staggering quantities. Dr. Henry Brill, chairman of the American Medical Association's Committee on drug dependence, estimated that from 1960 to 1970 the number of Americans who had sampled marijuana had increased from a few hundred thousand to 8,000,000. The majority of the new users ranged from 12 year old school kids to college seniors.[12]

A fourth and very significant factor promoting unrest and perhaps leading directly to the movement to force Donald Barr's resignation in 1970, came about as a result of his stance on the use of drugs by Dalton students: the drug problem, of serious national proportions, was equally severe, though on a lesser scale, at Dalton. "We consider marijuana a dangerous drug. We have found that most narcotic users have a desire to entice others into their situation. Narcotic use is, therefore, a contagious disease, and its control is a responsibility of the community."[13] To this end, Barr would expel high school students who brought drugs into the school or who sold, gave, or offered drugs to other Dalton students on or off of school grounds.

---

[12] Editors of Time-Life Books, *This Fabulous Century: 1960–1970* (New York: Time, Inc., 1970), vol. 2, p. 84.

[13] *Handbook: Dalton School* (New York: Dalton Archives, n.d.), p. 52.

Marijuana users might, at the discretion of the Headmaster, undergo therapy as a condition of remaining at Dalton; in any of these cases, the Headmaster would evaluate the evidence as to the student's involvement. Rules in the Middle School were similar, except that expulsion was at the discretion of the Headmaster; and if the child or parents came forth with the evidence first, the child would not be expelled. Furthermore, a child who had been using drugs would not gain automatic admission to the High School.

Few Dalton parents would question Barr's stance regarding drugs in general; however, many parents were distressed over the school's policy for users "after hours." And many parents did not regard marijuana as a dangerous drug.

Two final factors contributing to Barr's stressful years at Dalton were his positions on politics and on dress, both of which mobilized the parents to action and divided the parent body into two camps.

On November 14–15 in 1969, a Vietnam moratorium was planned which would interfere with the school day on Friday. In Barr's words, "political absences would be treated 'non-politically';" students who absented themselves would be subject to Saturday morning detention or "call-back." Donald Barr was a conservative in politics. He supported the war and had a son in the armed forces. His politics often rattled Dalton parents and students as he would freely share his ideas with them. Additionally, he supported a controversial, highly visible language teacher whose policies were much along the same lines as his own.

For a school which saw itself as valuing creativity and promoting self-expression, Barr's dress codes came as a shock. They affected both middle and high school students. They came at a time when youngsters had exchanged the "mod" look for the Beatles fashions: "the hairy, mustached, bearded, beaded, fringed and embroidered costumes of the late sixties."[14] Army surplus was soon to follow.

Again, Barr took a firm stance. In a letter to parents dated March 1, 1967, he stated that "Bizarre or eccentric costumes are more suitable to the stage than to the classroom, and faddism in clothing and hair-style is

---

[14]William J. O'Neill, *Coming Apart: An Informal History of America in the 1960s* (Chicago: Quadrangle Books, 1971), p. 238.

alien to the philosophy of the Dalton School."[15] In reply, some of Barr's constituents objected to dress codes on the basis that the school should concern itself with children's minds rather than with matters of dress and grooming, and that creativity should take precedence over costume. Barr retorted that "the child who thinks that creativity is indicated by oddity of dress is getting a poor start in life."[16] Specifically, the dress codes for middle school students were as follows:

> Boys may wear suits, or slacks with jackets, jerseys or sweaters. Slacks must be clean and pressed. Dungarees are not permitted. Shoes, not sneakers, are to be worn. Hair must be trimmed neatly. It should not overhang the forehead and in no case should come below the line of the eyebrows. It should not overhang the ears or the collar. It should be clean.
>
> Girls should wear dresses, or blouses and jumpers. Slacks, coveralls, or dungarees are not permitted. Shoes, not sneakers, are to be worn. Girls' hair should be clean and neatly trimmed and combed. It should not cover the forehead, and it must not reach below the line of the eyebrows.
>
> In the uppermiddle school, boys' hair is to be shorter and girls' skirts are to be longer: *The permissible length of a boy's hair is a matter for the School authorities to decide.* A girl's hemline is not to be higher than one inch above the knee.[17]

High school students also had acceptable modes of attire specified:

> *Dress*: Boys are required to wear a white or light-colored shirt and a tie; and a suit, or a sports jacket or blazer with suitable slacks. Dungarees are not allowed.

---

[15]Donald Barr, "Letter to Parents" (New York: Dalton School Archives, March 1, 1967), n.p.

[16]Ibid.

[17]Ibid.

Boys must wear shoes, not sneakers or boots.

Girls must wear dresses, or suits, or blouses or sweaters and skirts with hemlines not higher than one inch above the knee. Sneakers and barefoot sandals are not permitted. High-heeled shoes are unsuitable for many school activities.

Dirty or rumpled clothing is a sign of contempt for the School community. Students who dress unsuitably may be required to go home and change into acceptable clothing.

Boys' hair must be neatly trimmed and short. *The School decides what is short enough.* If the School authorities have to "suspend" a boy until his hair meets the School standards, this will be done.

Girls' hair must be neatly combed and arranged. It must not cover the face. It must not extend to the eyes.

We have noted with distress that some boys' and girls' hair is not clean. This is both unhealthy and unmannerly.[18]

The dress codes mobilized high school students. The dichotomy between freedom of mind but not of body was a difficult concept for Dalton students to accept, particularly at this historical moment:

We are treated as the cream of the crop of our generation—the Einsteins, Lenins, Joyces, and Renoirs of the future world—and yet we don't know how to dress ourselves properly. This assumption also contradicts a school policy of "freedom of mind."[19]

Students, however, while noting that "the headmaster's word was law," continued to violate the dress codes. The codes were difficult to enforce

---

[18]Donald Barr, "Letter to High School Parents" (New York: Dalton Archives, March 1, 1967), n.p.

[19]Marc Lebarle and Tom Seligson, *The High School Revolutionaries* (New York: Random House, 1970), p. 206.

because they did not have the complete support of the parent body and faculty. But they most certainly occupied the minds of students and perhaps afforded them a harmless outlet for their energies.

The specific events which led to the schism within the Dalton community and the tumultuous PTA meeting in the school's gymnasium on the night of March 15, 1970, have been chronicled in such popular periodicals as *New York Magazine* and *Time Magazine*. The former periodical points to a drug incident in which four middle-school students were counseled out of Dalton for using marijuana off campus, as the *cause celebre* that encouraged board members who were opposed to Barr's policies to take action to force his resignation. These trustees included Alfred Stern, a leader in the German Jewish financial community, John Jakobson, a Wall Street investment banker, Sara di Bonaventura, a member of the Roosevelt and Whitney families, Harris Huey, a respected parent within the Dalton community and, initially, E. Belvin Williams, a Teachers College Professor. Arthur Richenthal, a prominent New York lawyer and president of the board, led the counterattack.

As board members fought among themselves over the issue of whether or not to oust Donald Barr as headmaster of Dalton, their activities were "leaked" to the Dalton community at large. Thus the scope of battle was widened to include PTA leaders, parents, teachers, alumni and even students who quickly organized themselves into pro-Barr and anti-Barr factions. Of particular concern to the pro-Barr faction was control of three elected seats on the board of trustees: faculty, alumni, and PTA, all currently held by anti-Barr representatives. The strategy was to force the representatives to adhere to the will of their constituencies or resign. To this end, dinner parties were held, funds were raised, legal counsel was sought, especially by the Pro-Barr forces who appeared to be well organized, highly visible, and media connected.

Although difficult to document, it is highly likely that the pro-Barr camp was composed mainly of families who were fairly new to the Dalton community, while the anti-Barr camp reflected Dalton's "Old Guard"—German Jews, WASPS, serious artists and writers—more at home in the Dalton of Charlotte Durham than Donald Barr. Perhaps the anti-Barr faction felt excluded or eclipsed by the pro-Barr faction; perhaps the school was changing too rapidly and not necessarily in the direction the anti-Barr camp might choose. Whatever the case, the pro-Barr faction ultimately prevailed.

At the raucous PTA meeting on the evening of March 15th in the 89th Street building's gymnasium, the anti-Barr faction found itself under a carefully organized attack. At stake this particular evening was the PTA presidency, occupied by anti-Barr supporter, Dr. Myron Hofer, who by virtue of his office occupied a board seat. The objective of the pro-Barr supporters was to call for Dr. Hofer's impeachment and to replace him with Morris Levinson, a pro-Barr supporter.

In the unprecedented meeting that was immortalized in such periodicals as *Time Magazine* and *The New York Magazine*, several hundred Barr supporters angrily stamped their feet in unison on the gym floor, grabbed the microphone cords, hissed and booed anti-Barr speakers, thus rendering Barr's detractors impotent. These strategies proved successful. Dr. Hofer was impeached and replaced by Morris Levinson. Having met their objectives, one informant clearly remembers *Time Magazine* reporting that at the close of the meeting, participants "staggered out to their limousines and went home."

Donald Barr emerged from the fray of battle victorious. Subsequently, the board membership was reconstituted to reflect members favorable to Barr's conservative educational philosophy. Those who were opposed to Barr stepped down. Yet a scant four years after emerging victoriously from a battle which was publicized nationally as well as locally, Donald Barr resigned as headmaster of Dalton without any prior public indication of his intention to do so. What prompted this action?

The official reason given to the *New York Times* reporter, Gene I. Maeroff, was that Barr was in a disagreement with his twenty-member board "on the question of where the board's authority should yield to the headmaster's judgment."[20] Richard Ravitch, the board president at the time, agreed: "the issue is the prerogative of the board and the headmaster."[21] In particular, the board of trustees and the headmaster appeared to be deadlocked over two specific issues: whose prerogative it was to determine the necessity of and oversee an outside evaluation of the school and whose prerogative it was to determine administrative compensation and contracts. Both of these issues were addressed in the board of trustees meeting held on January 22, 1974, and in both instances, the board

---

[20]*New York Times*, February 7, 1974.
[21]Ibid.

overruled the objections of the headmaster.

In regard to the first issue, an outside evaluation of the school, the board was eager to appoint a committee to facilitate the matter. Barr objected. He questioned both "the expenditure of several thousand dollars when drastic cuts in the salary budget had just been announced"[22] and also "the timing, both as to its effects on the faculty after cuts had been made, and as to its informativeness before the cuts had taken effect."[23] Overiding Barr's objections, the board appointed a committee for the evaluation, consisting of trustees, Patricia Graham, Chair, Thomas Cooney, David Robinson, Susan Rolfe, and Camilla Rosenfeld. Fourteen members voted in favor of the evaluation; one voted against it and one abstained.[24]

Although Barr did his own evaluation of the school, particularly memorable to some informants for its wit, perception, intelligence and often insulting tone, such as referring to First Program teachers as "mini-skirted, plastic mommies with long red lacquered finger nails," the board committee on evaluation proceeded with their charge. Selected to evaluate the school were Philip Jackson, of the University of Chicago and former head of the Laboratory School (1970–1975), the progressive school in Chicago founded by John Dewey; Thomas Parker, Vice-President of Bennington College; Florence Howe, Professor of Humanities at State University of New York, Old Westbury and retiring President of the Modern Language Association. The evaluators were asked to focus on "ambiance, curriculum and organization at the school."[25] While each evaluator worked independently, nevertheless, the minutes further noted that certain general themes existed, particularly "administrative reorganization, curriculum review, scholarship funds, tone and morale."

Concerning the second issue, board of trustees president, Richard Ravitch proceeded to appoint three trustees, Robert Tishman, Chair, John Jones and Carol Sulzberger to serve on the Committee on Administration Compensation and Contracts. Again, Barr voiced his objection, stating that "the appointment and function of this committee was in violation of the by-laws in so far as it interfered with his authority to deal directly with his

---

[22]Board of Trustees, Minutes, January 22, 1974.
[23]Ibid.
[24]Ibid.
[25]Board of Trustees, Minutes, November 5, 1974.

subordinates in regard to their compensation and their responsibilities."[26] The board, however, did not waiver from its position and responded to Barr with the statement that, "the issue was not the responsibility of the employee but the form of contract."[27] Eleven trustees voted in favor of the committee, three voted against it and two abstained.[28]

Then, without warning, on February 15, 1974 Donald Barr resigned as headmaster of the Dalton School. Barr's resignation shocked The Dalton community. In response a special meeting of The Board of Trustees was held on Sunday, February 24, 1974 at 4:00 P.M. at the prestigious Harmonie Club. Twenty trustees were in attendance:

Mr. Donald Barr
Mr. Joseph Clark (left before adjournment)
Mr. Thomas Cooney
Senator Roy Goodman
Professor Patricia Graham
Mr. Timothy Knox
Mr. John Jakobson
Mr. John Jones (left before adjournment)
Mr. Thomas McCarter
Mrs. Olga Mack
Mrs. Midge Podhoretz
Mr. Richard Ravitch
Dr. David Robinson
Mrs. Susan Rolfe
Mrs. Camilla Rosenfeld
Dr. David Sidorsky
Mr. Gordon Smith
Mrs. Carol Sulzberger
Mr. Robert Tishman
Dr. E. Belvin Williams (arrived at 5:00 P.M.)[29]

---

[26]Ibid.
[27]Ibid.
[28]Ibid.
[29]Board of Trustees, Minutes, February 24, 1974.

Board president, Richard Ravitch announced that he had called the meeting in response to several members who wished to pursue more fully the reasons for and convince themselves of the irrevocability of Mr. Barr's resignation.[30] He further stated that the board should also address the issue of "a smooth transition and continuity until a new Headmaster is appointed"[31] and consider the creation of a search committee for a new headmaster.

In the ensuing discussion led by State Senator Roy Goodman and Mr. Thomas Cooney, Donald Barr was queried as to reasons for his resignation and whether his resignation was irrevocable. Barr responded, stating that he had no intention of withdrawing his resignation and "discussed at some length, the differences he felt existed between his conception of the duties and responsibilities of a Headmaster and that of the leadership of the Board."[32] Barr further stated that he did not believe these differences could be resolved and "repeated that his decision to resign was irrevocable."[33]

The issue of the Evaluation Committee created by the board was then raised. Barr stated that he did not object "to the Evaluation *per se*, but rather to the timing of it and the method of selection and presentation."[34] Following this discussion a motion was made to accept Donald Barr's resignation. However, before the vote was taken, Roy Goodman asked for a ten minute "recess" to talk with Barr. When the meeting resumed, a vote was called on the motion. Fourteen trustees voted in favor of accepting Barr's resignation; five members abstained.[35] The board then voted to create two committees: a search committee for the selection of a new headmaster and a search committee for the selection of an acting headmaster.

While the board of trustees in February determined to accept Donald Barr's resignation as "irrevocable" and move on to the selection of a new headmaster, nevertheless, as late as June 11, 1974, parents and faculty were still debating the issue and submitted their own petitions to the

---

[30]Board of Trustees, Minutes, February 24, 1974.
[31]Ibid.
[32]Ibid.
[33]Ibid.
[34]Ibid.
[35]One member arrived after the vote was taken.

board. The parent group's petition requested that the search committee formed by the board consider Donald Barr as a candidate:

> We, the undersigned Dalton parents, fear that the Board may not be aware of the strong desire of the parent body to retain Donald Barr as Headmaster of our school. We urge the Search Committee to take into account our expression of confidence in Mr. Barr's abilities as an educator by considering him a prime candidate for the headmastership.[36]

While the faculty, clearly in opposition to the sentiments expressed by the parent body's petition, urged the board "to go forward—not backward"[37] in selecting a new head of the school:

> We, the undersigned faculty members, express our support for the movement the school has begun to take toward a Dalton community in which the views and concerns of all members of the community (students, parents, teachers, administrators) are listened to and held in respect, so that a feeling of openness prevails. We feel that this educational policy can be achieved with a collegial model where advice is sought and respected by the head person who retains authority to make this final decision. In the past several years this atmosphere has not prevailed. We strongly urge the board of trustees to go forward—not backward—in seeking a head person who shares these goals and who has the educational philosophy and administrative style to implement them.[38]

It is telling that Barr's support came primarily from parents who, as I have stated earlier, found his hardline, conservative stance on dress and drugs particularly appealing amid the mayhem of the late sixties and early

---

[36]Board of Trustees, Minutes, June 11, 1974.
[37]Ibid.
[38]Ibid.

seventies. Perhaps it is safe to suggest that these same parents took comfort in Barr's more traditional rather than progressive approach to education; an approach that favored traditional demarcation of subject matter over integrated curriculum, and examinations and grades over project presentations and prose reports. In sum, an educational approach that would prepare students for life in the real world of cutthroat competition rather than for life on a hippie commune.

Telling too, is the fact that while the parents supported Barr, the majority of the faculty did not. Rather, they were critical of his style of leadership which, in his own words, was "rule by ukase." Perhaps this style might have been tolerated in a more traditional school at a different time in history; however in 1974 at Dalton, a school that had a strong tradition of respect for faculty opinion and for its inclusion in decision-making issues concerning curriculum and pedagogy, Barr's style was felt to be intolerable. Moreover it had not changed even though prior to the "civil war," many faculty members had been critical of his "highhandedness" and "inaccessibility." Rather, Barr's leadership style seemed to grow even more exclusive as if his victory signaled a vote of confidence for the restoration of the status quo ante bellum. Clearly, faculty expectations of change were at odds with the direction that the headmaster chose to pursue. As one faculty member remarked, it seemed to be a classic case in which "the operation was a success but the patient died."

Although the board of trustees did take the parent petition under advisement and did in fact offer a motion to engage a mediator "to seek agreement between the Board and Mr. Barr on the conditions, if any, under which his candidacy might be reasonably considered;"[39] it nevertheless, defeated the motion in a vote of fourteen to two,[40] following a lengthy discussion lasting two and one half hours. The board then voted on a motion which stated that since "no constructive purpose would be served in considering Mr. Barr as a candidate"[41] the search committee should move forward and assume responsibility for presenting possible candidates for the head of the school.

Although no records exist of the specific discussions at either the

---

[39]Ibid.
[40]Ibid.
[41]Ibid.

meeting of the board of trustees on February 24 or June 11, 1974 it is clear that by their actions, the majority of the membership wished to move forward and search for a replacement for Donald Barr. Again, while no records of discussion exist, nevertheless, there are certain concerns which emerge that might be construed as reasons for accepting Barr's irrevocable resignation. First and foremost is finances. If the sixties was a decade of political unrest, it was also a decade in which unprecedented fortunes were made. The seventies proved less succulent. Thus Barr, who had presided over a school which had experienced unprecedented growth and riches, now had to consolidate the gains made and cut costs across the board. This was not Barr's forte. Barr was, above all, an intellectual, more at home in a library than buried in a ledger. What the job now required was as administrator who could cut costs, balance the budget, while still delivering to students a first-class education. Although Barr had presided over a school that had grown tremendously to encompass three sites, nevertheless, he did not institute a rational form of governance for it. Rather, to many observers his way of doing business was thought to be that of reacting to situations as they presented themselves, rather than careful planning and rational implementation. In sum, the school in 1974 required a different type of head than Barr, one who possessed administrative skills rather than pizzaz. While Donald Barr had succeeded in making Dalton a "hot" school, nevertheless, his successor would have to assume the twin tasks of fiscal solvency and rational management in order to ensure the school's future. Whether or not this could be done in a manner consistent with Dalton's progressive heritage would be the challenge for the next head of Dalton.

Donald Barr's tenure as headmaster of Dalton ended in June, 1974. Peter Branch, the director of the High School was selected by the interim head search committee as acting headmaster. Then, in January of 1975, Gardner P. Dunnan, a school administrator from Briarcliff Manor, New York, became the next headmaster of Dalton.

7

THE DUNNAN YEARS (1975–present)

In January 1975, Gardner Dunnan became headmaster of Dalton. The American nation, scarcely beginning to recover from its involvement in Vietnam had just been traumatized by the Watergate scandal and the first resignation in its history of a president: Richard M. Nixon. In subsequent years, Americans would have to deal with recessions, declining economic dominance and global decline. By 1980, as a presidential election approached, Americans could only look back to the 1970's as a decade filled with problems both at home and abroad. It was in this context that Americans elected as their presidents, conservatives Ronald Reagan and George Bush.

Education, never immune to political, social, and economic forces, duly reflected the concerns of the American people. Gardner Dunnan became headmaster of Dalton just as the period of Larry Cuban describes as "informal education" was winding down.[1] From 1965 to 1975 "the tangled threads of social reform, child centered pedagogy, curriculum change, and self-liberation"[2] permeated public education. It was in this context that critics of public schools such as Jonathan Kozol, in his book, *Death at an Early Age* and Herbert Kohl, in his book, *36 Children*, branded schools as "mindless" and "destructive." Programs such as the "new math" and the "new science," introduced shortly after Sputnik had failed to live up to their promise. As education historian Diane Ravitch observes,

> The long heralded "revolution in the schools," prophesied only a few years earlier, had not come to pass; teaching machines, team-teaching, non-graded classrooms, and even the curriculum reforms supported by the National Science Foundation had not brought about the dramatic improve-

---

[1] For a more detailed discussion of this period see Larry Cuban, *How Teachers Taught* (New York: Longman, 1984), Chapter 4.

[2] Ibid., p. 150.

ment that was anticipated.[3]

Whereas Donald Barr insulated Dalton from the controversies and reform proposals of the period 1965 to 1975 in education, and indeed, might even be compared to King Canute who sought to hold back the Danes, Gardner Dunnan sought to introduce recent educational theory and practice to the Dalton faculty. To his credit, he encouraged the building of a professional library for faculty, encompassing such works as Joseph Featherstone's, *Schools Where Children Learn,* on British infant schools, Neil Postman and Charles Weingartner's survival strategies for teachers, *Teaching as a Subversive Activity*; Charles Silberman's immoderate book, *Crisis in the Classroom* and Paolo Freire's radical work, *Pedagogy of the Oppressed.* However, just as Dalton faculty began to become familiar with contemporary educational thought, Ravitch reminds us that, "Man: A Course of Study" or MACOS, an innovative social studies curriculum, developed by cognitive psychologist, Jerome Bruner, and introduced to the Middle School by Donald Barr, was being investigated by Congress. Organized around the life cycle of herring gulls, baboons, and Netsilik Eskimos, MACOS dealt with such subject matter as "infanticide," "senilicide", and "communal living"—subject matter too controversial for the American people in 1976.[4] Perhaps this was a harbinger of the conservatism of the 1980's, which was reflected in *A Nation at Risk,* the report of the National Commission on Excellence in Education, in 1983.

When Gardner Dunnan became headmaster of Dalton in January, the appointment came as a surprise to the Dalton community, which assumed that Peter Branch, the acting headmaster, would continue in his position for the full academic year which ended in June. Although there is much speculation as to why the appointment came mid-year, evidence suggests Dunnan was available, Dalton needed a headmaster, and the fit appeared to be a good one for both parties. It is interesting to note in passing that as in the former search for a head of school which culminated in the selection of its previous headmaster, Donald Barr, so in the latter, education historian, trustee, and parent, Lawrence A. Cremin was influential

---

[3] Diane Ravitch, *The Troubled Crusade,* (New York: Basic Books), 1983, p. 237.
[4] Ibid., p. 264.

in finding the school another head—this time while driving with Dunnan from Briarcliff Manor, New York, to New York City.

In addition to the speediness of Dunnan's selection another surprise was his training and experience as a public school administrator: a somewhat unusual background for an independent school head. Dunnan graduated from Harvard in 1962; he obtained an MAT in Science Education from Boston University and a Doctorate in Education from the Harvard Graduate School of Education in 1968. From 1967 to 1969 he served as an Administrative Assistant to the Superintendent in Shaker Heights, Ohio, implementing his dissertation proposal. From 1969 to 1974 he was an administrator in Briarcliff Manor, New York. Although Dunnan worked with elite populations in Shaker Heights and Briarcliff Manor, nevertheless, the bulk of his training and experience was in the public sector of education.

Otto Kraushaar notes in his work on independent schools[5] and Cookson and Persell suggest in their book, *Preparing for Power: America's Elite Boarding Schools*,[6] that the independent day school and especially the boarding school by design, produce their own leaders from among their ranks, occasionally from a university, such as in Barr's case or in the more recent examples of heads of Exeter and Hotchkiss, elite boarding schools. Moreover, independent schools tend to be insular and often impervious to significant educational reforms in the public sector. Dalton was no exception. Under Barr, in particular, Dalton teachers were not encouraged to attend conferences nor to use educational materials printed for "public consumption." As stated earlier, Barr openly denounced such important educational institutions as Teachers College, and purposely selected faculty who possessed degrees in the liberal arts over those who held degrees in education. Barr also sought faculty who had attended Dalton themselves, or other independent preparatory schools.

Furthermore, independent schools tend to be guilty of perpetuating the myth that they are superior to the public schools. Although there is

---

[5]A fuller discussion of those who teach and those who assume leadership positions in independent schools can be found in Otto F. Kraushaar, *American Nonpublic Schools: Patterns of Diversity* (Baltimore and London: Johns Hopkins University Press, 1972).

[6]Peter W. Cookson, Jr. and Caroline H. Persell, *Preparing for Power: America's Elite Boarding Schools* (New York: Harper and Row, 1985).

disagreement about research, in particular, sociologist James Coleman's recent work on private schools that supports this notion,[7] nevertheless, private schools have many advantages over public schools, such as a self-selected population and the power of expulsion. Whether or not this notion has merit is not the subject of debate here; what is significant is the prejudice Dunnan encountered given his public school background.

Dunnan himself notes that among his greatest accomplishments is that he created "order out of chaos."[8] Specifically, Dunnan encountered a school in which management was "sloppy" and "kids were being lost"; in which the rhetoric of child-centered progressive education of "students being responsible for their own learning really meant adult abdication."[9] Clearly, "educational matters and business matters needed tightening up."[10] However, Dunnan notes, that as he began to provide Dalton with orderly, rational management, he was (and continues to be) roundly criticized with, "But Gardner, it's so bureaucratic; it's so public school."[11]

Although Donald Barr had presided over a school that had more than doubled in enrollment during his tenure, little had been done to adjust management practices to the needs of a larger organization. Rather, Dalton continued to function along the lines of an organization in which policy was shaped through responding to problems as they presented themselves. As I have demonstrated, both in the cases of Helen Parkhurst and Donald Barr, this style of management in which heads constantly responded to problems without any rational plan ultimately contributed to their downfall.

While Gardner Dunnan did not implement a policy of long-range planning until fairly recently, he did dramatically alter the nature of the organization almost immediately after assuming his position as headmaster. In essence, the school had been run from its inception, as an informal organization in which personal loyalties functioned as an important strategy

---

[7]James Coleman, Thomas Hoffer, Sally Kilgore, *Public and Private Schools* (Washington, D.C. National Center for Education Statistics, 1981) and *High School Achievement:Public, Catholic, and Private Schools Compared* (New York: Basic Books, 1982).

[8]Gardner P. Dunnan. Interview, November 28, 1990.

[9]Ibid.

[10]Ibid.

[11]Ibid.

of control.[12] Dunnan did not abandon personalistic organization; rather, he introduced bureaucratic impartiality as well.[13] As sociologist Guenther Roth notes: the clever administrator uses *both* strategies of control: a mixture of personal loyalties and bureaucratic impartiality and the use of special emissaries with diffuse authority to carry out tasks that the rules and regulations impede.[14] It is precisely the combination of the two strategies: the mixture of personal loyalties and bureaucratic impartiality that Gardner P. Dunnan implemented from the start which both confounds and clarifies his leadership style.

The first major reform Dunnan implemented was the creation of a published pay scale for the faculty. In Parkhurst's and Dunham's eras, there was little discussion of salaries; money was not a genteel subject. As Otto Kraushaar notes in his discussion of faculty in independent schools, those who taught were assumed to possess either a Christian sense of mission or a trust fund or preferably, both.[15] Those who lacked the latter but were replete with the former scraped by, often tutoring on the side to supplement their meager salaries.[16] It is, however, interesting to remember that faculty during Helen Parkhurst's administration gave back a portion of their salaries when the school could not meet its expenses. Clearly, the early Dalton faculty possessed a sense of ownership, a sense of mission in Dalton's progressive experiment.

Money, however, became more of an issue under Barr, perhaps as the composition of the faculty shifted, perhaps as a reaction to the conspicuous consumption of the administration or perhaps as a general reflection of the times. Although entry level salaries existed and increments were publicly announced, salary negotiations were transacted individually and shrouded in a cloak of secrecy. Unequal financial remuneration abounded, particularly determined by social class and gender. Although difficult to document, it

---

[12]Randall Collins and Michael Makowsky, *The Discovery of Society* (New York: Random House, 1978), p. 124

[13]Ibid., p. 124.

[14]Ibid.

[15]Otto Kraushaar, p.143–171.

[16]Although teachers were (and continue to be) underpaid, private schools were notorious for paying teachers significantly less than what their public school counterparts were receiving, both in salaries and in benefits.

appeared that affluent married women as a group were discriminated against. One such informant told how, when discussing the possibility of a raise with her chairperson, a single male colleague, was told that her request was tantamount to taking the bread off his table.

Shortly after he arrived at Dalton, Dunnan proceeded to introduce a rational pay scale. Not only did it address inequalities, but it also served as a mechanism to determine or validate faculty credentials. Faculty were directed to place themselves on the appropriate step of the pay scale and to provide documentation to validate their placement. In addition to the pay scale, Dunnan subsequently created an elected faculty committee, Salaries, Benefits and Conditions of Employment Committee, and charged it with making yearly recommendations to the headmaster in those specific areas prior to his drawing up the budget for presentation to the trustees.

The second major reform Dunnan implemented was the creation of a hierarchical bureaucracy that would be responsible for running the school on a daily basis. To this end, Dunnan issued to the faculty an organizational chart with articulated responsibilities at each level. The structure was pyramidal: teachers at the bottom; senior teachers (formerly department chairs) at middle management level; curriculum coordinators to supervise both layers and report to the divisional directors who reported to the headmaster. Divisions were separated so that the Middle School had a separate identity from the High School; each had its own senior teachers, and its own faculty in social studies and English.

Shortly after the presentation of the new organizational structure, a Derby Day atmosphere ensued in which faculty jockeyed for positions of power. All faculty found themselves at the starting gate where former department chairs were pitted against other department members in a race for their jobs. Speculation as to who would become chairs, coordinators and divisional directors encouraged a spree of letter writing of suggestions for improvement to the headmaster. The spirit of cooperation—a hallmark of progressivism—was abruptly replaced by the spirit of competition, which appeared to permeate the school. In subsequent years, Dunnan created additional managerial positions. Among the most significant was the position of Assistant to the Headmaster for Curriculum (the coordinators were abolished) that Frank Moretti assumed in 1979. In 1988, the position was both elevated and expanded so that by 1991, Frank Moretti became the Associate Headmaster in charge of faculty and instruction. Frank Moretti came to Dalton—as did Barr and Dunnan—at the suggestion of Lawrence

A. Cremin. His experience was in higher education at New York University's School of Continuing Education. When Moretti came to Dalton, he encountered a situation in which, "the truth of the matter was that there was truly no job. I had to construct a position and did so with Gardner's help."[17] Moretti continues, "I looked for the problems. I did anything anyone asked me to do. I was entrepreneurial."[18]

Among Frank Moretti's measurable contributions to Dalton are the creation of a continuing education program; an expanded and institutionalized after-school program; introduction of the ICM Project in which teachers are trained in the investigation and communication method in science; introduction of archaeology projects in third and sixth grades, taught by archaeologists; introduction of the course "Philosophy and Practice" now taught by two former Dalton students. Moretti freely admits that Dalton was a new experience for him: "I was not accustomed to talking to people who had worked in one institution for twenty years; the territoriality was much more profound. My style was interpreted as aggression."[19]

While critics of Moretti point to his abrasive curmudgeon-like style, they admit that his position at Dalton is a difficult one and that his contributions have been valuable. Less measurable and perhaps most significant is the subtle role Moretti plays as the counterculture figure or "gadfly" of Dalton. One of Moretti's first public statements to the High School newspaper, The *Daltonian* highlights this role. Moretti, in an interview, voiced his criticism of secondary schools which "still cling to the pre-Darwinian notion that history, man and civilization began with Homer;" then he chastises them for emphasizing "mainly Western history and cultures," and in doing so, they are guilty of a certain degree of "indoctrination by omission."[20]

Another Associate Headmaster position was created for Frank Carnabuci in 1989, although one might argue that the position was an outgrowth of the numerous functions he had gradually assumed, first as an intern from Harvard; and later as Assistant Headmaster. Carnabuci's myriad responsibilities included (until he resigned in June, 1991) college counseling,

---

[17]Frank Moretti, Interview. Dec. 3, 1990.
[18]Ibid.
[19]Ibid.
[20]*The Daltonian,* November 23, 1982.

development, and alumni relations (the latter, a particularly sensitive area since Barr had alienated many of the alumni by not accepting their children), publications, public relations and school-wide admissions. Prior to his resignation, his staff included two full-time and three part-time employees.

Whereas Frank Moretti represents the social conscience of Dalton, Frank Carnabuci represents the social image of Dalton. As I have remarked earlier, one of Charlotte Durham's most significant contributions to the school was to legitimate it within the Association of Independent Schools. However, the conflicting tension between radical progressive education devoted to social reconstruction and child-centered pedagogy, and the impetus toward "respectable" Upper East Side independent school status continues to exist however uneasily. This tension is represented in the persons of Frank Moretti and Frank Carnabuci.

During the first ten years of Gardner Dunnan's administration, he continued to create additional layers of bureaucracy such as the Headmaster's Cabinet, which included Divisional Directors, Assistant and/or Associate Headmasters, Chief Business Officer, Director of Admissions and the Group; the latter consisting of middle management faculty, such as department chairs, grade level coordinators and First Program coordinators. The Group usually met for breakfast at 7:30 A.M. monthly to receive and disseminate information usually concerning Board of Trustees decisions. Several informants, highly critical of Dunnan's bureaucratic structure point to his growing inaccessibility and liken it to Donald Barr's. They suggest that Janet Pertusi, Gardner Dunnan's secretary, has assumed the role of gatekeeper similar to that role performed by Georgia Rice for Donald Barr. While Barr was inaccessible to faculty, and functioned through his group of "royal favorites," Dunnan functions through a well oiled bureaucracy which distances him from the average faculty member. Confusion is created, however, by Dunnan's style which is at times to invoke bureaucracy while at other times, to play the role of the *deus ex machina* and intercede when least expected. One informant in fact, suggested I measure the amount of space occupied by his administrators from 1975 to the present to gauge accurately the impact of middle management at Dalton. Interestingly enough, in August, 1990, in a letter to the faculty, Dunnan eliminated the Group meetings under the premise of "Less is more," the slogan coined by Theodore Sizer in his book, *Horace's Compromise*.

The third major task and one upon which the survival of the school hinged was creating fiscal solvency. Again, Dunnan's organizational skills and experience, particularly in the public sector of education where, as one informant observed, "financial control is all" were helpful in setting the school on a healthy fiscal course. Board of Trustees Minutes, especially documents lodged within the minutes from 1975–1978, speak to the financial miasma with which Dunnan had to cope. When asked ten years after he came to Dalton what he considered to be among his most important contributions to the school, he listed among the top, a published pay scale for the faculty and a balanced budget. To achieve the latter, he instituted a set of controls, which included a reorganization of the Business Office and strict accountability for spending. Dunnan personally signed each check over $1,000. Additionally, he requested and received daily budgets of cash flow generated from the Business Office and the Development Office. Computerized control of school finances was decentralized; a faculty development fund was created and a formalized accounting process for monies generated by High School Government committees was created. It is indeed ironic that what Dunnan is often criticized for, his public school-like organizational skills, is precisely what was called for at the time he assumed the headmastership of the school.

It is also obvious that Dunnan borrows heavily from sound corporate management practices. One example is the Kempner-Tregoe system of analysis of decision-making, used at Citibank. This process, as explained by Dunnan, is to "define your goals, establish which goals have not yet been solved, weigh the goals and then compare all the alternatives against the weighed goals." Another practice borrowed from the corporate sector is that of Long Range Planning. It was formerly articulated in a document entitled "Sometimes Performance is Performance" in May, 1988.[21] Specific areas to be addressed include, developing a rational planning process, strengthening the school's financial backing, increasing diversity among the trustees, upgrading the faculty, expanding facilities, diversifying the student body, expanding community service, and finally, exploring educational programs which would include multicultural concerns, environmental concerns and NYSAIS[22] critiques.

---

[21]This document was widely circulated throughout the Dalton community.

[22]New York State Association of Independent Schools, referred to as NYSAIS.

A serious criticism of the school, running through various evaluations from the 1970s through the 1980s is lack of space. In fact, space has been a serious problem at Dalton since Donald Barr's administration when the school more than doubled in size and became a coeducational institution through grade twelve. Thus, in 1977-1978 the Board of Trustees approved the purchase of 53 East 91st Street, the building adjacent to the First Program. Both buildings were then renovated; two floors were added and a gymnasium was built. In September, 1978 a newly expanded First Program opened, serving three year olds through third grade. In 1988 the Board of Trustees authorized the purchase of 52 East 92nd Street, a building contiguous to Dalton's First Program. The building was never renovated; rather it was resold and 63 East 91st Street, a town house adjacent to the lower school building was purchased instead.

Although it would now seem that the space needs of the school were met through this acquisition, this was not the case. Dalton, as most city schools, does not have adequate physical education facilities within its physical plant. Thus, students in the High School can only be scheduled for gym during the first and last periods; all "home" games, save basketball, have to be played "away"; students have to be bused to gym on 94th Street, or Randall's Island in the Middle and High Schools. And in a school of 1250 students, more space is needed for classrooms, music, and art facilities. Thus, the school directed its energies to acquire space for a new physical education facility which would free up space in both the 89th Street and 94th Street buildings. Both *The Daltonian* and *The New York Times* ran articles concerning Dalton's acquisition of four floors of space in a residential building on Third Avenue and 87th Street, which would house Dalton's 30,000 square foot physical education facility, a move first sanctioned by the Board of Trustees in 1989 in accordance with the Long Range Plan, to increase Dalton's facilities. According to *The Times* the school "raised the $10 million cost of its space, which includes $5 million for furnishings and fixtures, through donations and pledges."[23]

As a result of the Third Avenue commitment, there has been much speculation regarding the use of 8,000 square feet in the 108 East 89th Street Building and the facility used for gym—a former Con Ed Plant—on East 94th Street. Informants project that the total cost of renovation of the

---

[23] *The New York Times*, June 21, 1991.

present plant sites as well as the construction and furnishing of the new facility will run between $27 million and $32 million dollars. Thus, fund raising will assume new levels of importance in the near future.

In addition to the expansion of Dalton, there have been several other initiatives that warrant discussion. In the High School, the curriculum has been broadened to include study of non-Western cultures, particularly through the creation of the Interdisciplinary Department. The Investigation-Colloquium Method Project for Science and Mathematics was established, allowing Dalton students and teachers to work with students and teachers from other schools throughout the city for the expressed purpose of improving science and mathematics education in New York City. In 1986 Dalton joined the Mayor's Partnership for Public and Private Schools and Dalton continues to work with its partner school P.S. 130 providing tutorial support for its students. Dalton funds a lecturer at the Museum of Natural History; the school participates in the Black Rock Forest Consortium and has developed "environmental curricula" for use in public and independent schools.

Dalton's interest in international sites, beginning with Helen Parkhurst, continues through Gardner Dunnan's administration. High School students have participated in an exchange program with School No. 21 in Tallinn, Estonia, and with the Guangzhoo Academy of Fine Arts in China, the latter of which included a reciprocal exhibit of the work of students and faculty.

Chess at Dalton, especially in the First Program, has received a goodly amount of publicity since Dalton teams have won several national championships; in particular the 1985, 1986, 1987, 1988, and 1989 Primary School Team Championships. Learning chess, in fact has become part of the Kindergarten curriculum. Under former First Program director, Stanley Seidman, the program began in 1981 when Seidman brought Coach Svetozan Jovanovic to Dalton to teach and coach chess. "It's mental aerobics" says one educator; according to Seidman, it is an activity in which boys and girls can compete equally.[24]

An important innovation for faculty development is the introduction of endowed chair awards for faculty established in 1988. Not unlike the concept of merit awards for teachers, being debated nation-wide, the idea

---

[24]*Diversity and Excellence*, Annual Report, 1989, p. 18.

was first proposed in 1986 and was finally implemented in the winter of 1987–1988 when the first of twelve proposed chairs to be established was funded by investment banker, Saul Steinberg. The award entails a $10,000 increase in salary; in return, recipients must devote one month during the summer to curriculum development or other ideas relevant to the classroom. Applicants for endowed chairs must have taught full-time at Dalton for a minimum of five years; they must present a favorite assignment and their ideas about it; they must be observed teaching. A committee of seven make the selection; members of the permanent committee include the Headmaster, Gardner Dunnan, the Associate Headmaster, Frank Moretti, and the Directors of the Middle and High Schools. The first recipient in June, 1988, was English teacher and department chair, Andrew Glassman. While few would question the concept of rewarding excellence, nevertheless, its implementation does raise philosophical problems for a school that was founded on the concept of community and a school that fostered the spirit of noncompetitiveness in students and faculty alike. Another recent innovation, the Fisher-Landau Program, while somewhat controversial, is more in keeping with the original mission of the school.

The child-centered strand of progressive education that Dalton represented, helped to create a school climate that was particularly tolerant of individual differences. Many children who could be diagnosed as dyslexic today, in the Parkhurst and Durham years, were placed in progressive schools rather than in traditional schools since the former believed that education should begin with the needs and interests of the child. At Dalton, individualized instruction through assignments, labs and unit cards in the Middle School or progress charts in the High School encouraged and supported different learning styles, different levels of development, and different cognitive abilities. Progressive teachers such as Tessie Ross and James Hurst created assignments and classroom environments that nurtured, what Harvard psychologist Howard Gardner terms "multiple intelligences."[25] Children could work in groups or individually on projects; they could express their knowledge in a variety of ways: through art, music, dance, drama, as well as speaking and writing. They could master subject matter at their own pace and could be assessed, especially in the lower

---

[25]Howard Gardner, *Frames of Mind: A Theory of Multiple Intelligences*, (Cambridge: Harvard University Press, 1983).

grades, in a variety of nontraditional forms which emphasized creativity and individual expression. In sum, Dalton became a place where individual differences—physical as well as cognitive—were considered to be part of living, for Dalton attempted to be in Deweyan terms, "an embryonic community."

Dalton's philosophy and pedagogic practice allowed for a diverse student body to flourish. But this diverse population owed its composition in part to such gatekeepers as Mrs. Binger, Mrs. Cooke, and Mrs. Chapin, former Directors of Admissions, all committed to creating interesting often off-beat and artistic student bodies, yet providing a smattering of Upper East Side types as well to meet the payroll.

As the school expanded under Donald Barr, several informants concur that the student body, especially particular classes, became academically less able while the parents were more recently affluent. One informant in particular, notes striking parallels between fund raising campaigns and academically weak cohorts of students.

It is important to note that as Dalton became larger and more diverse in ability range, it also became more vulnerable to external pressures, such as demands for more academic rigor in the curriculum and in the quality of instruction. Then too, the school had to bow to the pressure of what sociologist Randall Collins calls "the credential society" in which one's cultural capital is defined by one's education, in particular, a diploma from an "Ivy League" institution.[26] As Cookson and Persell note, boarding schools, due to their longevity and geographic isolation are less influenced by educational fads and parental whims than day schools.[27] In particular, day schools such as Dalton, which have a predominantly female alumnae and/or meager endowment are all the more vulnerable.

Partially because of Barr's commitment to academic excellence, he introduced final examinations in the upper Middle School and examinations across the board, in the High School. He also was responsible for opening up the curriculum; for providing an elective system in the High School. To address the problem of a larger and more varied achievement level population, he introduced preceptors or tutors, who worked with students

---

[26]Randall Collins, *The Credential Society* (New York: Academic Press, 1979).

[27]Cookson and Persell, Chapter 2.

either individually or in groups. Originally there was a strong psychological component as well within the Preceptorial Departments in Middle and High Schools. However, with shifting personnel and different educational philosophies of headmasters, this latter emphasis has all but disappeared. Students were referred to preceptors through faculty or they could "drop in" on their own. This practice continues and the Preceptorial Room, especially in the High School, is usually full of students, and even more so around quiz and examination times. However, as many informants note, there has been reluctance on the part of students to avail themselves of preceptorial help because of the fear of being labeled.

While much of the above discussion may be repetitive, it is nevertheless important to recapitulate in order to understand that Dalton has historically made provisions for individual differences—in this case, ability—first through its child-centered philosophy and pedagogy; second, through the conscious creation of a particular faculty whose sole purpose was to address individual students' needs. This tradition was expanded in 1984, when the school received "a planning grant from the Fisher-Landau Foundation to explore the possibility of a project at the First Program for fifteen students with learning disabilities."[28] The following year, Dalton received from the same source, an additional $700,000 as "a two year gift."[29]

In sum, the Fisher-Landau grant allows for the mainstreaming of bright children with learning problems. It provides for

> early identification of children at risk for learning prob-
> lems, supportive mainstream intervention programs,
> educational programs to highlight strengths as well as
> remediate weaknesses and a coordinated and individualized
> educational program to support each child.[30]

Specifically the program includes nine major goals:

1. Early identification of students with learning problems.

---

[28]The Fisher-Landau Program at The Dalton School, p. 1.
[29]Ibid., p. 2.
[30]Ibid., p. 1.

2. Provision of individualized, educational programs within the students' classroom. (mainstreaming)

3. Provision of strategies for teachers to and in the identification and education of mainstreamed learning disabled students.

4. provisions of support and education for parents of learning disabled children.

5. creation of a multi-disciplinary team to diagnose, assess and monitor student progress.

6. provision of resources to facilitate an individualized and coordinated program for each student; this program would contain long term and short term goals.

7. use of specialists as consultants and resources to the classroom teacher.

8. emphasis upon language and speech development.

9. careful monitoring of student progress on an on-going basis.[31]

Located in the basement of the First Program and under the directorship of Susan Etess, a former Middle School social studies teacher and a former Middle School director, it is probably one of the few true vestiges of the Dalton Plan as Parkhurst conceived it, due to its commitment to "recognizing individual styles and encouraging team work."[32] Clearly, I would agree with Gardner Dunnan's statement in support of the Fisher-Landau program that "Part of Dalton's heritage as a school is to plan for the

---

[31]Ibid., p. 3–4.

[32]Andrea Fooner and Shirley Longshore, *Growing Together* (New York: Dalton School, n.d.), p. 66.

individual differences among students,"[33] and that Fisher-Landau provides this service.

However Dalton has not "come full circle" as Dunnan claims by linking "the roots of our school" with "the needs of an individual child (Louise Crane) with learning problems whose family was struggling to provide her with a quality education to meet her individual needs."[34] Louise Crane, Mrs. W. Murray Crane's youngest child, was not learning disabled; she was instructed by Parkhurst for one year and when her family left Dalton, Massachusetts, for New York City, she was sent to boarding school.[35]

Support for implementation of the Fisher-Landau Program was not overwhelmingly positive. Etess notes that at first the Board of Trustees rejected the grant because they feared "Dalton would become a school for the learning disabled."[36] According to Etess, the Board capitulated when members understood that many of the children who would be eligible for Fisher-Landau were already at Dalton; furthermore, many were children of Board members. Parents opposed to the program capitulated when they realized that their children would receive extra help and not be counseled out of the school.[37] Dunnan, in *Growing Together* is particularly candid in discussing issues surrounding Fisher-Landau that made the Board Members initially reluctant to accept the program. Specifically, he points to concern for the school's reputation, its academic standards, its curriculum, its admissions, and its undermining of the faculty's self-confidence.[38]

Informants from the Dalton community, queried on Fisher-Landau offer mixed opinions regarding its efficacy. It appears to work best in the First Program, where the program is located and where the children are least stigmatized by the label of Fisher-Landau. It is less successful in the upper grades, where there is less structured support, and where parents are more concerned with the effects of labeling on college admissions.

What does emerge in regard to the discussion of programs, such as

---

[33] Ibid., p. 8.
[34] Ibid., p. 8.
[35] Interview with Chester Page, September 11, 1991.
[36] Susan Etess, Interview, December 8, 1990.
[37] Ibid.
[38] Fooner and Longshore, p. 63.

the Preceptorial Department or Fisher-Landau—programs designed to meet the needs of individual children within the school—is the widespread practice of outside tutoring. In a poll administered to 322 out of 400 high school students, 195 of the respondents reported that they received tutoring, "not only...for standardized tests but in order to pass or raise their grade in a course as well."[39] Former Director of the Lower School, Stanley Seidman, reported that "even two year old students are coached for their nursery school interviews."[40] Moreover, he voices concern that this practice "sets them up so early for a lifetime of grade-oriented pressure."[41] Other administrators, such as former High School Director David Arnold, raise concerns that rampant tutoring indicates that the Laboratory System is not working; he and other faculty members as well point to grave social class distinctions created by tutoring. Most students state that they are just victims of the system and that they have no choice but to follow the trend if they are to remain competitive with their classmates—namely regarding their scores on the PSAT's and SAT's[42] and their class rankings.

While Fisher-Landau and the Preceptorial Department may not address the concerns of parents and students seeking cultural capital, nevertheless, they remind us of the school's original commitment to diversity. Enrollment at Dalton as of the school year, 1990 was 1,256; of the entire school, 18% receive scholarship assistance; 9% receive full assistance, and 9% receive partial assistance. Of the 18% receiving scholarships, 21% are attending the High School. According to Dunnan "the 1989-1990 academic year witnessed the largest number of minority and scholarship students in an entering freshman class in the history of the Dalton School."[43]

High School students have addressed the issue of minorities at Dalton by organizing a series of Diversity Meetings which culminated in an assembly during the school year, 1989-1990. The consensus of opinion was that the student body must be made aware of what it is like to be a minority

---

[39] *The Daltonian.* March 18, 1988.
[40] Ibid.
[41] Ibid.
[42] Ibid.
[43] *Diversity and Excellence*, 1989 Annual Report, p. 4.

student at Dalton; also, that the student body address issues of multicultural-ism. Although Dalton is far from exemplary in its commitment to "the other America," nevertheless, there has been a genuine effort from its beginnings to create a school culture which would, in Dewey's words, "mirror society."

An important activity which serves to illustrate the school's reaching out to the community was that of Community Service, performed by high school students during Parkhurst's and Durham's administration. Community Service lapsed during the seventies; however, it was reinstated in the High School as a mandatory requirement for graduation by the then director, Stephen Clement during the academic year 1980–1981. Closely monitored by a coordinator of community service, students perform tasks such as working in soup kitchens, tutoring at the Storefront School in East Harlem, working with the disabled and/or elderly and walking dogs at the ASPCA. Reaction to community service has been mixed. Its former coordinator, Peter Perretti believes that it is essential to the experience of every student in order to increase the feeling of being a member in the community.[44] Two Dalton students, after the first year of community service received awards from the Yorkville Community Center; one for work with the hungry; the other for tutoring. However, not all students favor the program. In particular, one senior, highly critical of community service observed that "It's so obnoxious. It reeks with noblesse-oblige. It's like 'We the fortunate of the world will help those less fortunate just to fulfill a requirement. It makes me ill.'"[45] Indeed to many students, community service has become yet another credential to add to their profiles for college admission. Nevertheless, whatever the motives, community service acts as a vehicle to sensitize affluent, and often insulated students to the problems of disadvan-taged New York City residents.

A recent and important innovation in curriculum and pedagogy at Dalton, one which clearly indicates the importance the current administra-tion attaches to technology is the project "Education for the Twenty-first Century." Founded on the premise that multi-media systems will replace

---

[44]*The Daltonian*, October 19, 1981.
[45] Ibid.

traditional modes of instruction in communication and computation,[46] it seeks to prototype a new system of education, one based on the intensive use of multimedia information technologies as the primary means of access to the cultural content of education.[47] The project generated the creation of New Laboratory for Teaching and Learning at Dalton, funded in 1991 through a generous gift of two million dollars from a former Dalton parent and trustee, Robert Tishman. The program of instruction includes *Archaeotype* a program in which students,

> work in small groups to excavate a section of a simulated archaeological site. As they dig and discover things, they send them to the simulated lab where they measure, weigh and begin their research into the nature of their specific discovery. They are encouraged to use both the resources within the library of the program as well as other resources outside the orbit of the program such as museums, experts and library materials. The challenges built into the project are intentionally multidisciplinary...[Students] are called upon to make inferences about the society and culture of the site...they are encouraged by the team-oriented nature of the archaeological enterprise itself to cooperate with each other to achieve this goal.[48]

Interestingly, *Archaeotype*, a computer program developed in 1990–1991, and in particular, designed for sixth graders studying Ancient Greece, contains significant elements of progressive curriculum and pedagogy, namely problem-solving, integrated curriculum and cooperative learning. Other projected projects include *Ecotype*, which

---

[46]"The Cumulative Curriculum: Multi-media and the Making of a New Educational System" (New York: Institute of Learning Tehnologies, Teachers College, Columbia University), September 8, 1991, p. 15.

[47]Ibid., p. 43.

[48]Mary Kate Brown, Luyen Chou, Neal Goldberg, Frank Moretti, "Archaeotype: Discovering the Past through simulated Archaeology" (New York: The New Laboratory for Teaching and Learning, The Dalton School), 1990–1991, p. 1.

> will engage the students in thinking as naturalists, as they
> gather new information about flora and fauna, having to
> classify, to understand ecological relations, and to chart
> potential human activities and responsibilities in the
> classroom. This project will involve classroom based
> interactive simulations, as well as on-site research in the
> facilities of the Black Rock Forest.[49]

This program certainly reflects an attempt to meet an important goal articulated in the Long Range Plan, to explore educational programs which would include environmental concerns.

While Dalton, through the New Laboratory for Teaching and Learning is working as an individual school, nevertheless, it views its role in developing an integrated or "Cumulative Curriculum" as one in which the school "will be doing its part to develop a model of a more humane, effective education than others can adopt in coming decades."[50] To this end, the school is involved with the Institute for Learning Technologies at Teachers College, Columbia University, the Cooper Union Research Foundation, the Lab Schools of District Two and The New York City Mayor's Public-Private School Partnership in seeking "to collaborate with IBM Watson Research Labs in a basic development program designed to achieve systematic innovation in education through the use of advanced information technologies."[51]

It is predictable that reaction among faculty to the New Laboratory for Teaching and Learning is mixed. Enthusiastic users of multi-media technology for classroom instruction endorse it as a welcome addition designed to enhance classroom instruction. Others, however, voice skepticism over the claim that multi-media technology will eclipse book learning and view the New Laboratory as "glitz" or window-dressing, designed more for image than substance. Interestingly, one informant who was considering working on the project was not impressed. On the contrary,

---

[49]"New Laboratory for Teaching and Learning: A Proposal for Technology and Education" (New York: The Dalton School), July 15, 1991, p. 7.

[50]Ibid., p. 1.

[51]"The Cumulative Curriculum," p. 1.

he felt that what Dalton was beginning to embark upon was already being done elsewhere.

In May 1989, in what is probably the most controversial move in Dalton's history since it expanded and became coeducational through the High School, the Board of Trustees members voted to eliminate the First Program's Nursery and Pre-Kindergarten programs.[52] Thus as of 1991, the age of the youngest Dalton student has been five years.

Statements from the headmaster reveal that there were two overriding concerns in the Board arriving at its decision:

> ...admissions criteria are not suitable to determine the potential long term success for a three year old (the school does not admit additional students to the four year old pre-kindergarten program), and that the small size of the nursery grades require that Dalton disappoint many families despite its inability to fully defend the admissions process, leading to negative publicity and ill feelings about the school.[53]

Dunnan noted in an earlier interview in *The Daltonian*, the especially high rejection rate: of thirty-six children admitted each year to the nursery program, two hundred or eighty-five percent of those who apply are rejected.[54] Furthermore he underscored the ensuing negative publicity: "people say if they don't get in I'm not friends with so-and-so, it must be because I don't have a lot of money, it must be because they only want this sort of kid."[55] In the same interview, he pointed out that decisions on admission of older children were more easily explained; that test scores, observations and reports from an applicant's previous nursery school allow "you to have something to talk about."[56]

The decision was not arrived at unanimously at first. In the April meeting of the Board, the vote was evenly split and Dunnan refrained from

---

[52]*The Daltonian*, May 12, 1989.
[53]Ibid.
[54]*The Daltonian*, March 17, 1989.
[55]Ibid.
[56]Ibid.

casting the decisive vote. Rather, to resolve the April 11 tie vote of eleven to eleven, the Board was instructed to submit individual written ballots to resolve the matter no later than April 19.[57] In the final count, "seventeen members voted to abolish, while nine voted to maintain the nursery programs and four members abstained."[58]

Those opposed to the elimination of the nursery program cite three compelling reasons for its retention. First, that Dalton is only one of two schools in the region to admit children at such an early age and that this affords Dalton a particular distinctiveness; second, that early admission to Dalton allows for the building of a community from the earliest years and third, that the nursery program is an important tradition that should be maintained.[59] Former Director of the First Program, Stanley Seidman, stated "I am disappointed because I see the nursery as an important part of the First Program."[60] Parents, such as Linda Franks, who wrote about her child's experiences in the *New York Times Magazine*, was also a vocal opponent, and many parents signed a petition against the abolition which she sponsored.[61] Most faculty at the First Program opposed the change as well.

Although Dunnan has emphatically stated that the decision was primarily motivated by an attempt on the part of the school to dispel its "undeserved negative reputation"[62] surrounding the rejection of two and a half year-olds, nevertheless the issues of space and money cannot be discounted. Although the school's total enrollment will remain at approximately 1250, the elimination of the nursery program would allow the fourth grade to move to the First Program, thus freeing up valuable space in the 89th Street building and addressing the New York State Association of Independent Schools (henceforth referred to as NYSAIS) recommendation leveled at both the High School and Middle School in 1984 that, "the school—led by the Board of Trustees and the Headmaster—continue its

---

[57]Gardner P. Dunnan, Letter to the Board of Trustees Concerning the Nursery Program Phase-Out, April 12, 1989.

[58]*The Daltonian*, May 12, 1989.

[59]Ibid.

[60]Ibid.

[61]Ibid.

[62]Ibid.

vigorous, imaginative search for increased space to house Dalton's academic, cultural, and athletic programs."[63]

Then too, there is the issue of money. The elimination of the nursery program and the school's commitment to a total enrollment of 1250 will allow for an increase of four students per grade, thus generating considerable additional income for the school, since tuition rates are lowest in the early grades.

To be fair to Dunnan, he did state in *The Daltonian*[64] that the school had been considering eliminating the nursery program fifteen years ago and that he would conduct a review of the decision during the 1994–95 school year: "If I feel we're losing kids to Horace Mann, we'll reinstate the program." "On the other hand," said Dunnan with a distinct laugh, "On the other hand, we often get students from Horace Mann's nursery and I love that."[65] Interestingly, in a memorandum to the Board of Trustees on March 6, 1990, from the Headmaster, the first item addresses what was apparently an unpopular proposal, that of moving the fourth grade to 91st Street: "We will terminate the portion of the Plan (Long Range Plan) that includes moving the fourth grade from 89th Street to 91st Street."[66] Thus, the configuration of the Middle School remains grades four through eight.

While the nursery program is being phased out, nevertheless there is considerable concern that,

> Dalton's current enrollment is an "inevitable pyramid."
> That is to say we have the smallest cohort of children in
> the youngest group with a gradually increasing grade size
> as one moves up through the school. We should change this
> profile to a "rectangle" by admitting more students in the
> First Program and reducing significantly over admissions

---

[63]New York State Association of Independent Schools (NYSAIS), Office of the Headmaster, 1984, p. 100.

[64]*The Daltonian*, May 12, 1989.

[65]Ibid.

[66]Gardner P. Dunnan, "Memorandum to the Board of Trustees", March 6, 1990.

in the Middle School.[67]

To alleviate this imbalance and to address the problem of losing families who applied to kindergarten, Dunnan proposed adding twelve additional kindergarten students which would

> ...allow us to offer up to 20 additional kindergarten contracts to the families that we are currently reviewing. It is our firm judgement that if we do not enroll these families at kindergarten they will be admitted at other excellent schools in which they will succeed and they never again consider coming to Dalton.[68]

Remaining competitive to other "excellent schools" thus appears to be the overriding rationale for enlarging the early grades. Noticeably absent is any mention of the commitment progressive educators, such as the founder of Dalton, Helen Parkhurst, had to early childhood education. Perhaps, if more attention had been paid to the school's progressive roots, a stronger case might have been made for the retention of the nursery program. Certainly, the ambiance of the First Program will change and the focus of instruction will become more academic in nature, thus mirroring the concerns of the "excellence movement" in education: a movement away from the progressive and most recently, the "informal educators" (1965-- 1975)[69] who were concerned with the affective domain of the child and toward the conservative educators who emphasize the cognitive domain of the child and who are concerned with academic rigor, a national curriculum and standardized tests to measure achievement. Thus in the larger context, the elimination of the nursery program, dubbed "Baby Sitting" in the *Daltonian*, can be seen as a sign of the times, ushered in by *A Nation at Risk*, which has dominated educational thinking over the decade; a document

---

[67]Gardner P. Dunnan, "Memorandum to the Board of Trustees" (New York: Dalton Archives, February 13, 1990).

[68]Ibid.

[69]See Cuban, *How Teachers Taught*, Ch. 4.

that conjures up "a full-scale invasion of Sonys, Hyundais, and Tele-funkens"[70] on America's shores; that takes Americans to task to losing their economic supremacy to the Japanese in particular, and squarely places the blame upon the nation's schools. While Dalton is an independent school and can therefore retain far more autonomy over curriculum and pedagogy than a public school, nevertheless, each administration reflects (or in Barr's case, attempted to deflect) to some degree, the educational thinking of the times. Interestingly, Dunnan seems to have moved from *Teaching as a Subversive Activity*, to *A Nation at Risk*, with relative ease:[71]

> In 1990, the School will celebrate the 70th year of its founding. Thus, while it is inevitable that we should look ahead, and plan for the education of students in a society that is more complex ethnically and culturally, it is enormously reassuring to be able to do so from the vantage point of an institution that has more than lived up to the hopes and dreams of its founders. *With total confidence, I can report to you that Dalton's concern with excellence is more than a commitment. It is a goal we have achieved.* ...Our task is to guarantee that we continue to offer excellence to future generations of Dalton students.[72]

The students, as well as the administration, reflect the new wave of conservatism sweeping the country. Even though issues of alcohol and drugs, AIDS, and cheating on exams proliferate, the driving force of a great many Dalton High School students is gaining admission to a *very* select college, preferably an Ivy League institution, and succeeding in business. Concerning the latter, an important and telling event was an assembly of Wall Street notables, co-sponsored by Dalton and the Riverdale Country

---

[70]Joseph W. Newman, *America's Teachers* (New York: Longman, 1990), p. 236.

[71]Readers should note that Postman and Weingarten have since repudiated their radical stance in *Teaching as a Subversive Activity* in the 1980s.

[72]Gardner P. Dunnan, "Letter From the Headmaster," Diversity and Excellence: 1989 Annual Report (New York: Dalton School), 1989, p. 4.

School, held on May 15, 1991 at Dalton. Addressing students, parents and faculty, Alan Greenberg, C.E.O., Bear Stearns advised the audience on the best strategy for getting a raise "...have a competitor offer you a raise. Your own employer will grant you one right away;"[73] Roy Furman, President and C.E.O., Furman Selz, admonished students, "Don't be homogeneous—go out on a limb: learn an oddball language such as Lithuanian. You'll be hired because you stand out from the crowd;"[74] Andrew Tish, Chairman and C.E.O, Lorillard delivered, "the ten commandments of turn-around management;"[75] and Lawrence Small, Chairman of the Executive Committee, Citicorp/Citibank urged students, "to go into business, government, art or education, all of which are vital for everyone concerned."[76]

Regarding the former point, the overriding concern with college admissions, tutoring (as previously noted) abounds. Students in the High School, as early as grade nine go off to Stanley Kaplan to prepare for the Biology Achievement. The equation, it seems, is that excellence = achievement = Eastern establishment (preferably Ivy League) college or university. The Admissions catalogue, the *Alumni News* and *The Daltonian* all prominently display college destinations of Dalton graduates. The following list, shows colleges "most frequently" attended by Dalton graduates from 1985 through 1989:[77]

Amherst	14	NYU	10
Barnard	5	Northwestern	10
Bennington	4	Oberlin	10
Boston University	5	Princeton	18
Brandeis	3	Sarah Lawrence	3
Brown	40	Skidmore	5

---

[73]Nina Rothschild, "Big Business: Four Financial Leaders Speak to Students," *Alumni News* (New York: Dalton School), Winter 1990/91, p. 10.

[74]Ibid., p. 23.

[75]Ibid., p. 10.

[76]Ibid. p. 23.

[77]The Dalton School Admissions Catalogue, (New York: The Dalton School, n.d.), p. 29.

Bryn Mawr	5	Smith	3
Clark	3	Stanford	6
Colgate	3	Swarthmore	7
Columbia	8	Syracuse	5
Connecticut College	3	Tufts	19
Cornell	32	Tulane	3
Dartmouth	7	U. of Chicago	5
Duke	13	U. of Michigan	6
Emory	7	U. of Pennsylvania	28
Franklin & Marshall	7	U. of Southern Ca	3
Georgetown	12	U. of Wisconsin	3
Hamilton	6	Vassar	18
Harvard/Radcliffe	37	Washington U.	6
Haverford	4	Wesleyan	21
Johns Hopkins	3	Williams	3
Middlebury	7	Yale	31

In light of the emphasis placed upon academic achievement and college placement, the Dalton Plan, the linchpin of the school Helen Parkhurst founded, begs examination.

As I have demonstrated in the previous chapters, the Dalton Plan has undergone a transformation from the days of Parkhurst through Barr. The Dunnan administration has made significant attempts to preserve elements of the Plan, however, size of school, conservatism of parents, society's emphasis upon credentials and leadership's reluctance to swim against the educational tide of excellence—all of these elements mitigate against preserving the Dalton Plan. Nevertheless, the NYSAIS evaluations completed in March, 1984 note that the components of the Dalton Plan: House, Lab and Assignment are introduced in the First Program in varying degrees and "provide a basic structure for the education of the young, (however) they are most clearly visible in the higher grades."[78] Most clearly visible in the First Program is House which is described by the evaluators as "the classroom setting" and the House Advisor as the

---

[78]Report of the NYSAIS Evaluation Visiting Committee, Office of the Headmaster, March 1984, p. 1-2.

teacher.[79] For the First Program students, the Assignment,

> ...a contractual agreement between the student and the teacher—"a primary supplement to daily class and homework"—is introduced in the Second Grade, where given at first on a weekly basis, "it outlines for the student a problem or area to study, suggests ways to research and solve the problem, while providing options for satisfying its requirements"[80]

Laboratory time in the First Program, according to the NYSAIS evaluators, "is often classroom worktime, during which students pursue any of the areas of study for which they have contracted with the teacher or work independently on group assignments."[81]

Clearly, the Dalton Plan in the First Program operates primarily through the House, which serves the function of allowing children to perform both as individuals and as members of a group, realizing their individual potentials, yet allowing them to experience "group life." Secondarily, the Assignment which begins in second grade, allows the children to begin to learn how to budget their time and teaches them responsibility.

While the First Program at Dalton may seem progressive to visitors to the school, and may be progressive in comparison to other independent schools, it is not progressive, notes Seidman, "in terms of Dewey and Parkhurst."[82] For example, far more mixed grading existed under Parkhurst than at Dalton today; then, too, in Parkhurst's school, it was possible for students to work on a single project for an entire year.[83] What *is* progressive about the First Program today continues Seidman, "is the way in which it encourages autonomy. There is a willingness to let kids become independent and grow on their own; there is much more freedom for

---

[79]Ibid., p. 2.
[80]Ibid.
[81]Ibid.
[82]Ibid
[83]Ibid.

kids."[84]

Of the three divisions of Dalton, the Middle School appears to be the most successful in utilizing the Dalton Plan although, according to the NYSAIS evaluators, who visited the school in 1985, "The committee was both impressed by and disappointed by the three essentials of the Dalton Plan, House, Lab and Assignment. The applications of these essentials varied enormously from teacher to teacher. Some teachers were devoted to all three; others avoided one or more."[85]

House in grades six through eight, consists of a single grade, usually fifteen to sixteen students in size, and meets either in the mornings or afternoons depending upon the grade level, two times per week for fifty minutes. Students check in in the mornings with House Advisors between 8:10-8:20 A.M.; they check out in the afternoons, "just like a pit stop," according to one informant. In grades four and five the House Advisor is also the student's Social Studies, English, or Math teacher, and House meets daily. In the "Lower Houses," attention is given to providing the House Advisor more time to work with his/her own students. The consensus among informants is that House "is a real thing regarding the House Advisor and the student but it is not connected to the community anymore."

House Advisors introduce Middle School students to Laboratory time or Lab. Lab times are scheduled into the child's schedule, usually two periods per week. This works well if the teachers the students need to see are free; however, the nature of Lab time has evolved from an extension of the class (i.e., enrichment), to remediation without ensuring that students in need of help will find their teachers accessible. Teachers do have the option, however, of turning one of their class periods into Lab since classes meet four times per week, and one of those times is a double period.

According to one informant, the Assignment, "has never been what it was supposed to be," and that the Assignment should consist of:

1. an assessment or pretest to determine what the student knows;

---

[84]Ibid.

[85]Report of the NYSAIS Evaluation Visiting Committee, Office of the Headmaster, June, 1985, n.p.

2. goals set directly after the assessment, which articulate what the student will master;

3. tasks which will allow the student to master the set goals;

4. an assessment, or post-test to determine if the goals were mastered.

In a document entitled "Assignment on the Assignment," however, the Assignment is articulated somewhat differently:

(1) requirements which reflect an awareness of different levels of student ability as well as of different learning styles;

(2) themes and approaches which make possible the interdisciplinary synthesis for which Dr.(sic) Parkhurst called;

(3) clear but not overbearing directions which stimulate reflection, inquiry and an authentic encounter with human questions and creates occasions for student-faculty (Labs) and student-student discussions.[86]

Obviously there is some divergence between the reality of practice inherent in the first description and the rhetoric of the second document, which needs to be put into practice. The bottom line about Assignments, as one informant notes, is that when kids are sick, mothers call up and ask for homework and books. Nowhere is it in the minds of these kids or parents that the *homework* is the Assignment. Thus the question teachers pose, both in the Middle and High Schools (and the one that goes unanswered) is, How can they internalize the Assignment within the Dalton community?

According to an issue of *The Daltonian* which features articles on the Assignment, it is equally problematic for students and teachers in the

---

[86]Frank A. Moretti, "Assignment on the Assignment," February, 1987.

High School. One article in particular points to the way in which Assignments vary in quality from class to class; that some teachers really utilize them while others don't. In particular, one teacher, "hands out assignments at the beginning of each unit and says, "Here's more toilet paper for all of you."[87] Another article points to the under-utilization of the Assignment by students. A preceptor in the High School notes that,

> When I ask to see an assignment, I generally get an unwrinkled, pristine assignment never before consulted, and from this I conclude that the assignment seems more a peripheral than an integral part of a student's life. I do not remember the assignment evolving from an individualized, often utilized contractual agreement between student-teacher body of material, but for whatever the reason, I currently see the assignment as less of a contract and more of a calendar of events.[88]

While others concur that the Assignment in the High School has become a "calendar of events," one student interviewed, voiced the opinion that the Assignment functioned as a vehicle for measuring the accountability of individual teachers to the curriculum: "Currently, it (the assignment) is used to outline a student's work for an extended period of time. I feel that it is also used to keep the teacher on the right path in class."[89] Furthermore, the student continued,

> the fact is, that the function of the assignment has decreased severely over the last decade. What once played a major role in the student/teacher relationship of a Dalton education is now only a symbol. It is used as an excuse to assign more homework under the pretense that the student (sic) ration their time in advance so that they have ample time for their work.[90]

---

[87]*The Daltonian*, May 1, 1991.
[88]Ibid.
[89]Ibid.
[90]Ibid.

It is not only the Assignment that is problematic in the High School. The NYSAIS report of the visiting committee to the school, April 13-April 16, 1986, suggests that "The Dalton Plan of House Lab and Assignment be vigorously reexamined....at the moment, Dalton is not consistently or fully maximizing the use of this creative concept."[91] Furthermore, the visiting committee recommends that the school look to the schedule in the High School and determine whether or not it is conducive to the Dalton Plan; that the school "determine which aspects of the progressive legacy of Helen Parkhurst...are viable today" and devote school-wide faculty meetings to this discussion; that new faculty be subject to monthly meetings to discuss "what they have learned about The Dalton Plan and how it works."[92]

House in the High School is as troubling as is the Assignment, since formerly House functioned as an important link for students to the Dalton community. House in the High School has varied from single age grading to mixed age grading and although the number of students has remained constant at about sixteen, its composition, time slot, and even purpose have varied, especially since the High School has been subject to five different directors from 1975 through 1991. While younger students seem to have more of an allegiance to House, older students, plagued by the nagging reality of college admissions, appear to play down House. Thus it may primarily function as a conduit for information from teachers to students concerning their progress or disseminate information; secondarily, it may function as a vehicle for sharing school-wide concerns or policies. According to the NYSAIS report, House has indeed strayed from its original intent, which was to function as "the *primary* social unit of the school." Thus, the evaluators urge that the Dalton High School, restore the House Plan to its original function...; develop a curriculum that takes advantage of the informal, nonthreatening forum of the House; and support House Advisors with in-service programs.[93]

House is not a course and students do not receive grades per se; rather they receive House reports, and therefore, House attendance in the High School has been problematic. The time slots for House have been

---

[91]NYSAIS, "Report of the Visiting Committee," Office of the Headmaster, April 13-April 16, 1986, pp. 58–59.
[92]Ibid., p. 3.
[93]Ibid., p. 34.

experimented with; sanctions for missing House have been imposed, then dropped; thus ultimately, attendance in House may depend upon which homework assignments are due or whether or not the House advisor exudes charisma or wields power within the community (i.e., whether the House advisor is also the headmaster or a key administrator in the High School).

Lab, the final component of the Dalton Plan, has also come under attack, first because of the shrinking amount of Laboratory time students actually have and second, because of the way in which it has been reinterpreted. One significant adjustment Dunnan made when he became Headmaster, was to move from a three-day, sixty-minute class schedule in the High School to a schedule of four days, forty-five/fifty minute periods, thus reducing both the amount of Lab time for students and the actual availability of teachers. One informant noted in particular that she felt that "there was a perception on the part of the Headmaster that Dalton teachers weren't working hard enough and needed to be scheduled into more classes." Many faculty members point to the high energy level teaching at Dalton requires, and indeed, one eloquently voiced the opinion that "Dalton is not just a job. It's an encompassing way of life." Nevertheless, a feeling of lack of trust in the faculty often prevails. Thus, a policy which may have been implemented as a result of shared faculty between divisions of the school or of particular schedule concerns may be seen as containing a hidden agenda. Whatever the intent, the reduction of Laboratory time and the introduction of more classes inexorably altered the concept of Laboratory time.

In previous administrations, Lab functioned as an extension of the classroom. It could be individuals meeting with teachers to discuss topics not broached in class; it could be group labs, organized by students who had similar lab times. Lab was a place to explore ideas although it could be a place for clarification as well. Today, however, informants note "the concept of lab has been remedial—it's a stigma to go to Lab." Furthermore, students interviewed in the March 18, 1988, issue of *The Daltonian* point to the futility of going to Lab, since the same person explains again, in the same language, what you didn't understand the first time in class. Some students, of course, continue to use Lab wisely but again usually for clarification or as one informant noted "to haggle over a grade on a paper or exam." Clearly, as the NYSAIS group indicates, the components of the Dalton Plan have to be reexamined in light of the demands of the schedule, and perhaps within the context of the different educational and societal concerns that originally inspired Helen Parkhurst to create her progressive vision, the Dalton Plan.

Evident in this chapter, is the fact that Dalton has undergone a further transformation from Barr to Dunnan. Thus it is necessary to pose the question, what is the ethos, "the enduring values or character of the school community"[94] that emerges during the administration of Gardner P. Dunnan? Informants agree that "clearly the school is a reflection of the personality of the principal"; Also, that "there is little institutional memory." Rather, the Dalton Plan is often dredged up "to justify our educational priorities." The consensus is, however, that for Dunnan, "the central value is change." One informant offers three words to describe the Dunnan administration: "change, flexibility, movement." Another source urged as I described my book project to her, "Quickly write it before it changes." That Dalton has indeed changed since 1975 when Gardner P. Dunnan became the headmaster of a financially troubled, poorly managed, independent school with a progressive tradition is evident. But the school, as I will argue in the following chapter, not only reflects the personality of the headmaster; it is influenced by a larger configuration of teachers, parents, neighborhood, community, and societal concerns. And as progressive education has waxed and waned in educational circles, so has the Dalton Plan with its three components: House, Laboratory, Assignment.

*   *   *

In concluding this chapter, I realize that of all the heads of Dalton I have said the least about Gardner Dunnan's personal style and philosophy of education. That he has created a rational bureaucratic model comes through loud and clear. That he is first and foremost, the final decision-maker is not always as evident; in part this is masked by his bureaucracy; in part this is due to his low-key affable, personal style.

Board minutes and correspondence reveal Gardner Dunnan's setting agendas for committees of both trustees and faculty. Indeed, it is Dunnan who approaches the Faculty Salaries, Benefits, and Conditions of Employ-

---

[94]Gerald Grant, *The World We Created at Hamilton High* (Cambridge: Harvard University Press), 1988, p. 172.

ment each year to tell the committee what it should reasonably expect and therefore, request in the way of a raise. It is Dunnan as well who will dismiss editors of the student paper or its faculty advisor at his discretion, or even a divisional director. What comes through is the fact that a mechanism exists for running the school but the head in this case, nevertheless, exercises his authority as he sees fit.

Discerning Dunnan's educational philosophy is more difficult task due to the ever changing, somewhat trendy nature of the slogan he adopts for the school each year. Clearly, from the reading he encouraged the faculty to do, when he first came to Dalton, Dunnan was very much influenced by the revival of progressive education, as defined by Diane Ravitch, or of informal education, according to Cuban. Shortly after he arrived, he invited educational historian, trustee and parent, Lawrence A. Cremin, to address the faculty. Predictably, Cremin urged the school to act boldly and return to its progressive roots; that in the end, colleges would continue to accept Dalton students, just as they had in the Eight Year Study agreement. Further, he urged that Dalton join with other schools and refuse to grade students; rather, assess them through prose reports without grades—the standard report format of Parkhurst and Durham's administrations. This has not occurred, although there has been serious discussion recently in the high school of eliminating advanced placement classes, which often results in tracking and competition.

What has occurred in the school has been a concern for academic rigor and accountability. To these ends, the High School has been transformed into a serious, demanding environment in which students in required courses follow common assignments and take common exams. It has become a place where on any given day, visitors to the fifth or sixth floors of the school, predominately high school floors, will witness teacher-centered traditional style pedagogy in action. Sadly, one informant who attempted to be faithful to progressive pedagogy reported that she was accused of not teaching her class by her former chairman, because when he walked by her door, he did not see her in front of her class. Rather, she was sitting among her students in a circle, a practice he was obviously unfamiliar with.

It is telling that the NYSAIS evaluation of the High School recommended that the school:

1. encourage the writing of assignments which truly reflect the individualized learning thrust of the Dalton Plan and

find ways of sharing well-written assignments among departments on a regular basis.

2. restore the House Plan to its original purpose as the *primary* social unit of the school; develop a curriculum that takes advantage of the informal, non-threatening forum of The House; and support House Advisors with in-service programs.

3. explore ways in which the faculty could demonstrate the continuum of knowledge rather that the fragmentation of learning.

4. examine and be cognizant of the priorities in the schedule to determine if it accommodates the principles of the Dalton Plan embodied in the Laboratory and House Plan.[95]

In a similar report directed to the Middle School, NYSAIS evaluators,

observed too much teacher-centered instruction, too many drill sheets, too many blackboard and chalk talks, and too many "discussions" that were really "teacher-student" and "teacher-other student" dialogues. We did see imaginative teaching and student involvement in learning, but Dalton should have more of it, for Dalton is a special place.[96]

That Dunnan has encouraged his faculty to form committees to explore assignment writing, pedagogy, etc., following the evaluations is a fact. Also, under Frank Moretti's tutelage, a course on the philosophy of progressive education has been added to the curriculum for high school students. Nevertheless, as previously mentioned, an informant reported that

---

[95]NYSAIS Report of the Visiting Committee to the High School, Office of the Headmaster, June, 1986.

[96]NYSAIS Report of the Visiting Evaluation Committee, Office of the Headmaster, June, 1985.

new teachers often think that the Dalton Plan is some form of medical insurance benefit. Thus, attempts to address the NYSAIS critiques may be only partially successful.

In sum, Gardner Dunnan has had to cope with running a financially troubled school, bringing to it a rational form of organization, attracting a steady flow of applicants to its doors, placing its graduates in prestigious colleges and universities while also addressing the pressing need for diversity, for permanent funding and for space. The question unanswered here is this: would it have been possible to address the myriad problems of the school and to have maintained its progressive philosophy as well? Clearly, Dunnan has created a school whose graduates attend some of the finest colleges and universities in this country. Clearly, his administration represents a success story but at what cost to the school? The lesson Dunnan offers to progressives is a disturbing one, for he has demonstrated through his administration that survival may necessitate some form of compromise with the school's progressive roots. It is possible that progressive education, such as the Dalton Plan, may not be feasible given the current constraints under which the school operates and that it is best to forget the past. Although copies of an article appearing in the *Phi Delta Kappan*, entitled "To Teach Responsibility, Bring Back The Dalton Plan" were circulated by the headmaster's office to the faculty, thus far, the homage paid to Dalton's progressive roots seems more rhetoric than reality. Whether this is due to a reluctance of the headmaster to commit himself to an educational philosophy which may be unpopular and may prove unfeasible is not to be determined within this book. However, it may well be the example of Dalton indicates that progressive education in its original philosophy and practice may have to be drastically altered if it is to survive.

8

THE FACULTY

As the whole can be no greater than the sum of its parts, so Dalton can be no greater than the people who interpret its ideal. No matter how world-shaking an idea is, it will be of little value if the people who expound it are not also great. A school in the final test is no greater than the faculty that makes it live.

To this end the Dalton School has continually obtained vital, stimulating people as its teachers. Many of the faculty have been attracted of their own accord to Dalton, others have been sought out....But one thing stands out in all members: their personal devotion to students and the school. The Dalton faculty is one of the busiest faculties in the nation. With private lives of their own they attend many faculty meetings to plan the future of the school, to integrate their courses and to consider the individual classes. They take part in the Student Government, extra trips, projects and individual attention, besides their sincere belief in the value of their subjects, make courses live in the students' eyes. And "the faculty" are appreciated by students for many informal contacts—the drugstore, house meetings, house parties, committees, ski trips and the like, constantly affirm the fact that they are human beings who enjoy being with us.[1]

No history of the Dalton School would be complete without a discussion of some of the men and women who constituted its instructional staff and who were responsible for giving the institution its particular flavor on a day-to-day basis. From its inception through today, Dalton has been blessed with

---

[1]Marilyn Moss Feldman, ed., *Dalton School, A Book of Memories* (New York: Dalton School, 1979), p. 28.

a talented, colorful faculty. Helen Parkhurst, Charlotte Durham, Donald Barr, and Gardner Dunnan all had in common a faculty that was "high powered, volatile, full of prima donnas."[2] Each had respected the individual differences of teachers as well as the individual differences of students. As will become evident, "diversity in experience, in talent, in temperament, in intellect and in attitude"[3] were present in the section of teachers from Dalton's beginnings. I think it also a fair assumption that the selection of teachers reflects the individual preferences of the heads, as well as the needs of the school. Thus, the tone, set by the head, is reinforced through his/her staff.

If I were to present a generalization regarding Dalton's staff, I would have to agree with Otto Kraushaar's portrait of an independent school teacher, "that of a dedicated amateur—a man or woman broadly educated in the humanistic liberal arts tradition, not highly specialized, and but lightly burdened, if at all, with the pedagogical formalism of professional education."[4]

And these dedicated amateurs—men and women who served to form a link with the past and carry out the traditions established by the founder of the school—subsequently participated in amplifying, modifying, or abolishing the same practices and traditions they helped implement.

Before looking at some individual profiles, however, it must be pointed out that Dalton teachers, as teachers in an independent school, had many "advantages" over their counterparts in the leading competitive public institution, P.S. 6. They could formulate their own curriculum; they had considerable leeway in the implementation of that curriculum; their class sizes were smaller; their students were carefully screened in a selective admissions process. And, until the school became as large as it is today, relationships between faculty and administration were far less formal—more on a familial basis. Teachers were virtually free from classroom supervision until Donald Barr created the position of department chairman and introduced the evaluation process.

It is also true that teachers at Dalton were not required to be certified. It is interesting to note that many of them did, in fact, possess

---

[2]Ibid., p. 6.
[3]Barth, p. 26.
[4]Kraushaar, p. 145.

M.A. degrees from Teachers College, Columbia University, or from comparable institutions, indicating that they may have been state certified. But unlike their counterparts at P.S. 6, they did not have to submit to written and oral examinations administered by New York City's Board of Education. This was viewed as a positive attribute since, "In the selection, the independents give more weight to the candidate's education in appropriate subject fields and to personal qualities,"[5] such as "character."

Who are the faculty members archetypical of the administrations of Helen Parkhurst, Charlotte Durham, Donald Barr, and Gardner Dunnan? It is difficult to state definitely since Charlotte Durham inherited many of Helen Parkhurst's staff members and was able to maintain them throughout her tenure as head. Additionally, because she assumed the role of head during Parkhurst's many absences , her tenure, among many observers, was regarded as an extension of Parkhurst's.

I believe, however, that there are discernible differences between the two administrations and have stated what I think they are in Chapter 4. It then follows that there are discernible differences between faculty members who came to Dalton during the "pioneer" period and faculty members who came to Dalton in the period of "stability." For example, let us begin by looking at one of Dalton's formidable and beloved prima donnas, Elizabeth Seeger. Elizabeth Seeger came to Dalton in the fall of 1922. In her own words, she recounts her interview with Helen Parkhurst and the subsequent circumstances she encountered regarding her employment:

> I had been interviewed, the previous spring, by the head of
> the school, Miss Helen Parkhurst, who looked at me
> searchingly with her large, rather visionary eyes and asked,
> I believe, a few questions. A kind providence decreed that
> the subject I was engaged to teach was history, for I was
> not properly qualified to teach anything and history had
> always been one of my great interests. I found, on report-
> ing for duty, that my "laboratory" was one-thirds of which
> was devoted to science, divided from mine by a glass
> partition. I also found that I was to teach seven grades,

---

[5]Ibid., p. 322.

from the fourth through the tenth. There were five girls in
the high school: three in the ninth grade, two in the tenth;
they seemed very grown-up and rather intimidating. There
were three little girls in the sixth grade; the other grades
were normally populated with boys and girls. An easy job
for the teacher, you think? O yes, but remember that there
were seven assignments to be written every month and that
one should acquire at least a minimum amount of information about the subject matter contained in them: that is, for
me, the history of the western world, from Egypt and
Babylonia up through modern Europe. The next year we
added a year of Oriental history, for which we had to write
not only the assignments but the books, there being none
available.[6]

Although Elizabeth Seeger proved to be a brilliant teacher and
talented author, she was quite accurate in stating that she was "not properly
qualified to teach anything." Her educational preparation, noted in the
Trustees and Faculty Handbook (1955–56), was Brearley School. Her
experience: District School No. 5, Union Vale, New York; the Dalton
School.
Seeger proved to be both adaptable to the vicissitudes of Dalton and
dedicated to making the experimental school "work." In addition to her
teaching, she wrote five children's history books: *The Pageant of Chinese
History*; *The Orient, Past and Present*; *The Five Brothers—The Story of the
Mahabharata*; *The Pageant of Russian History*; *Peter The Great*. In her
foreword to *The Pageant of Chinese History*, written in 1933, which I chose
to include here so that the reader may get a more personal glimpse of her,
she reveals her rationale for writing the book:

Ten years ago I was asked to teach History in a
progressive school in New York City. The curriculum that
I was concerned with, which covered the five years from

---

[6]Elizabeth Seeger, "Memories of the Children's University School," *The
Dalton Bulletin* (New York: Dalton School Archives, 1968–69), p. 26.

the fourth to the eight grades, was, to my mind, the most right reasonable one for children to follow. They started their study with the earliest known civilization, that of Egypt; this led naturally to the other ancient empires of the Near East, then to Greece, to Rome and to medieval and Renaissance Europe. Then they followed the great discoverers to America and spent two years on the history of their own country. It was a continuous, logical story and an excellent preparation for the study of modern history in high school. But there was one great gap in it. The Far East, with those great nations whose vivid and dramatic stories and whose religions and civilizations are such an important part of our world, was entirely left out.

This, of course, was not peculiar to any one school. It is only lately that such a broad curriculum as this that I have mentioned has been available to children. But since we wanted to make it truly comprehensive, and since the headmistress of this particular school had a great love for the East, as I had myself, we decided to include at least a year of Oriental history, in the sixth grade, and to go eastward, as well as westward, with the great discoverers.

So I began to look about for books that twelve-year-old children could study. There was an adequate little history of Japan; but, although good books may have escaped me, I found nothing, either good or bad, for India and China. We had not time, unfortunately, for more than these three countries. At that time many general histories were being published, stories of the "World," and of "Man" and so forth. Considering their titles I looked hopefully at these; but alas! In books of fifty or sixty chapters one or two were devoted to the farther countries of Asia. Books for adult readers were little or no better. General histories of civilization, art, philosophy, literature and so forth, arc still being written with no mention of the unsurpassed achievements of the East. What a strange disproportion is this! After all, it is close to seven hundred years since the Polos made their way to Cambaluc, and more than four hundred since Vasco de Gama sailed to

Calicut. How long are we going to look at every aspect of human life with only one eye?

Besides the practical need of knowing about these great nations that are still so strange to most of us, we can ill afford to lose the intrinsic interest and beauty of their histories. Surely, though perhaps I speak with partiality, there is no history more thrilling and delightful than that of China. I cannot agree with some writers who state that the interest of Chinese history begins with foreign relations, or who give one-fifth of the space in their books to China before A.D. 1500 and four-fifths to the rest of its history. If it were not for very recent developments I should be more inclined to say that the interest of the history ended with foreign relations. It is the Chou Dynasty, which began in 1122 B.C., with its astonishing visions of social life, its philosophy, its dramatic events and its subtle and humorous anecdotes, that richly repays the student. It is the adventurous and inventive dynasty of Han, the magnificent renaissance of the T'ang and the exquisite art of the Sung dynasties that delight the soul even more than the later history. But all the thousands of years of the nation's growth are a mine of interest and enjoyment which has been only partially opened to us.

To return to our school problem. Finding no books for our use, I was constrained to write a sketch of Chinese history for the children myself, while my friend, Dhan Gopal Mukerji, wrote a similar sketch of the history of India. With these, which were often revised and enlarged, the history of Japan, and a correlative course in Oriental literature and dramatics, the children became as familiar with the history and thought of Asia as they were with those of other continents and loved them as well. The present volume, though it does not pretend to be a textbook, is an amplification and a completion of the sketch begun in school.

No one is better aware of the presumptuousness of the task or of the inadequacy of this book than its writer. The history of China is more like the history of a continent than that of a nation, and its very length demands a rigorous selection of material. I have tried, as far as I am able, to take the Chinese point of view rather than that of Western commentators. Out of a mass of events I have followed those that form a consecutive and simple narrative, and out of wealth of legend and story I have chosen those that seem to symbolize important aspects of Chinese civilization. Much that is valuable has, of necessity, been omitted; I have stressed certain things, and have touched others very lightly. I trust that other books will soon supply what mine may lack, and that we shall have as many histories of China for children as we have histories of nearer but no more interesting or important lands. I set forth this volume as one might a decoy bird, hoping that it will attract winged and living comrades to its side.

For any fault in book or author I have only two excuses to offer: the immediate need, both for adults and children, to know more about our great Eastern neighbors, and my own deep love and admiration for the splendid history and culture which it has been my joy, as well as my task, to study.[7]

Another paradigm of a Parkhurst teacher is Harold A. Thorne, "Thornie," whose domain included shop and theatre arts. Thornie possessed adaptability, talent, commitment, and style, prerequisites for working for Helen Parkhurst. He was a Welshman, educated at University College, London, the University of Toronto, and the Mechanics Institute in Rochester, New York. His experience, prior to coming to Dalton, included teaching at the Harley School in Rochester—private classes in puppetry and crafts in Rochester, scenic construction for summer stock. Thornie worked first for Helen Parkhurst, then for Charlotte Durham. He says of Parkhurst:

Our Headmistress and Dalton Founder—she was a terror to work for. Indefatigable and with gray gimlet eyes, she

---

[7]Elizabeth Seeger, *The Pageant of Chinese History* (New York: David McKay Co., 1934), pp. vii–ix.

scared everyone including the Board of Trustees. I loved
her even though I was afraid. I felt, thought, that if we had
a good Pageant with fond parents and loving relatives with
tears in their eyes, my job was safe for another year.[8]

When Thornie came to Dalton, there was no Drama Department.
He and another teacher, Mrs. Mildred Geiger, created it by mandate from
Helen Parkhurst. The early days were chaotic and challenging, as Thornie
collected "a crew of would-be carpenters and electricians" to construct
theatre equipment for school plays. Thornie reminisces of the old days:

> The theatre was hard work; no matter how much
> time we had to rehearse and get the settings ready, there
> was always something we could do to improve the produc-
> tion. But schools, plays, and pageants are marvelous. One
> has a sympathetic audience and rarely are these flops. And
> it is always nice to hear "oohs" and "ahs" and "oops" of
> praise and to agree how wonderful so and so was. It
> happens every year.
>
> Working in that sort of atmosphere one is apt to
> forget the many successes that the children of Dalton have
> given you. So forgive me if I tell you a few of the howlers.
> Like the time someone bumped into a large tree trunk
> which started to fall into the front of even second row. We
> sent a crew member out to catch it and stand behind as
> balance until the end of the scene. Then there was the time,
> I think in "The Devil and Daniel Webster," in which there
> was a setting in a stable or a blacksmith's. Anyway half the
> set we let down from the flies and forgot to pull it up for
> the next act. And then there was the classic time which was
> completely my fault. Some Greek play, in which the
> victorious army sacked the town and the final curtain
> showed the winning general standing on stage with his
> officers. The setting—flames from the burning town with

---

[8]Harold A. Thorne, "Reminiscence," *The Dalton Bulletin* (New York:
Dalton School Archives, 1968–69), p. 29.

smoke crystals dropped in an electric heater with the smoke wafted by a fan. I goofed; plugged in the heater and fan too soon—result, everyone choked nigh unto death on stage and the smoke drifted out in the house and even the front hall!!

Another high spot in my life was Mrs. Mukerji. What a marvel. Her Indian and Medieval plays, many originals, written by the class. Fifth and Sixth Grades I expect. One Indian play had twenty-seven scenes and I think each scene ran shorter than it took the crew to set it up. Those plays were grand, with half the lines being ad libbed and I never knew when to pull the curtain. As the time when opposing armies had six men each and there was heavy slaughter—and no curtain. Finally about ten corpses cried to me, "Thornie, the curtain, The Curtain."[9]

At Christmas time Thornie became ubiquitous, helping supervise the Christmas Pageant, Helen Parkhurst's "production of the year." A lighted cigarette dangled from his lips at all times, in defiance of the no smoking regulations around the students. His language was spiced with Anglo-Saxonisms and was highly picturesque; Thornie was always a source of amusement.

Elizabeth Seeger and Harold Thorne are Dalton "greats." They reflect the pioneer spirit of Helen Parkhurst, her unorthodox approach to running a school, and her eccentric personality.

Although Charlotte Durham managed to maintain many of Parkhurst's teachers, she nevertheless selected faculty members who reflected both her own rigorous academic preparation and rational yet "progressive" approach to teaching. Two quintessential examples of her administration are Tessie Ross and Hortense Eugenie Tyroler.

Tess Ross, known to her students as "Tessie," taught social studies in the fourth and fifth grades during Charlotte Durham's administration. She was Chairman of the Lower Middle School from 1956 to 1962. Tessie was educated by the nuns in a formal convent school in Brussels, Belgium. She attended the Ecole Normale de l'Etat and then the University of Brussels.

---

[9]Ibid.

Tessie taught at a public school in Brussels; she then became an instructor at Brussels Belgium Labor College. In the United States, she worked at the Little Red School House, Manumit School, and Hessian Hills School—all "experimental" schools. While fourth and fifth grade students at P.S. 6 were studying the regional geography of the United States and the explorers, Tessie's students at Dalton were studying history, beginning with the Hebrews and the Egyptians in the fourth grade; continuing with Greece and Rome in the fifth grade. And when Tessie's students studied the Hebrews they *became* slaves unto Pharaoh for the day, bound to one another, engaged in building a pyramid.

In 1987, shortly after her death at the age of 83, the Dalton School held a memorial tribute to Tessie Ross. Fred Hechinger, a former Dalton parent and longtime *New York Times* education writer, wrote a moving tribute to her in one of his columns. Titled "Gift of a Great Teacher" it captured both the type of teacher that Tessie Ross was, as well as the type of progressive school Dalton was under Charlotte Durham, and to a lesser extent under Donald Barr and Gardner Dunnan. Hechinger writes:

> Tessie is different from the other teachers", a 9 year old boy told his parents at dinner. When he was asked how she was different, he replied, "Tessie knows how we children think."
>
> Tessie, the boy's fourth-grade teacher at the private Dalton school in New York, was Theresa Ross, who taught elementary and middle school classes for nearly 60 years- 43 of them at Dalton. Last June, Tessie, who was affectionately known by that name to children and adults alike, died at the age of 83. Several generations of her former pupils and their parents will pay tribute to her at the school on Thursday.
>
> The only way to describe great teaching, a rare art, is to study great teachers like Tessie. When her pupils recognized that she knew how they thought, it did not mean that she herself thought childishly or indulgently about them. To write about her is not to celebrate a person but to try to define some of the qualities of exceptional teaching.
>
> It has been said that education is what you remem-

ber when you have forgotten what you have learned. Often that means remembering one's great teachers more vividly than any particular lesson. Anyone who has never had at least one such teacher is truly deprived. To expect many is unreasonable. I remember three. The most memorable taught first and second grade. Even at the age of 6, without being told, I sensed that he was a true artist. Children know this.

The children knew this about Tessie. Doctrinaire conservatives might have looked on her with suspicion. She was an early disciple of John Dewey, whose child-centered progressive views still raise a red flag in many minds. Worse, a native of Brussels, she had been a member of the Belgian Socialist Party.

As a teacher, her only doctrine was to make education come to life. When she taught history, her favorite subject, she took the children back with her into antiquity. She believed that even fourth-graders could deal with the universe.

Joan K. Davidson, now president of the J.M. Kaplan Fund, a charitable foundation, was a student teacher in Tessie's class. She recalls how Tessie used all the children's experiences to teach them—street games, the previous night's television programs, great myths.

She would do "weird" things, Mrs. Davidson recalls. To make children understand the evil consequences of a hostile invasion, she once had her pupils "invade" another classroom. As expected, the result was bedlam, and she asked the children to report on the experience.

Great teachers are strong enough to dare being unconventional, even controversial, and this was an example. Actually, says Carol Cone...[former] head of Dalton's middle school, Tessie had second thoughts about the experiment and never repeated it. Still, both she and the children had learned from the experience.

Popular myth has it that progressive education is dangerously permissive and leads to low standards and chaos. Tessie's idea of progressive education was, like

Dewey's, that the school should function like a well-ordered, fair community. Mrs. Davidson, whose four children' were Tessie's students, recalls: "She never allowed kids to be mean to each other. And she would not tolerate disruption."

Mrs. Cone, who came to the school 23 years ago, remembers Tessie as "the teacher who guided me most." She taught her that every child must be given a chance to be a leader and a follower.

Great teachers develop their own ways, without relying on prescribed lesson plans. Tessie said: "The child needs a framework within which to find himself; otherwise he is an egg without a shell. The adult is there to guide and teach. If a child asks how to do something, you don't tell him just to go and find out; you say, 'come, let's work it out together.'"

She could be tough. Once, a little boy arrived in class without his assignment and told Tessie he had left it at home. She took him by the arm and started to go home with him. He confessed that he had not done the homework. It never happened again.

"Children must learn that any act has its consequences," she said. She considered it absurd to teach ethics separately from other subjects.

"She'd let children know when she disapproved," a former colleague recalled. "She had a gesture with her hands that said something like, 'I'm going to cut your throat' and it usually was enough. She never prejudged children, never thought of them as being below grade level. She looked at their progress."

She loved taking the children on an annual trip to a farm in Massachusetts, but Mrs. Cone remembers there was always learning along with the fun. One year, after the children had been reading about the flooding of the Nile in Egypt, they created and observed miniature floods.

Once, a picnic in the park that she and her fourth-graders had prepared was rained out, to universal groans. Tessie's response was to have the desks and chairs pushed aside, turning the classroom floor into a substitute picnic ground.

Tessie tried to get children to understand the nature of leadership without lecturing about it. She might start with baseball or with the news, and then move on to Julius Caesar.

One test of great teachers is how long their influence lasts. Many of Tessie's former pupils would come back to her for advice in the crisis of later years—in high school, in college, and as adults. Her advice was never indulgent. Should a college student take a year off, just to relax? "I believe in finishing what I started, and enjoy myself afterwards," she would say.

One of the optional courses Tessie created was "The Characteristics of Growth," and she taught it until she died. In it, seventh-and eighth-graders worked as assistant teachers in the nursery school and kindergarten. Afterward, she discussed with the students how children behaved, how they learned and grew.

When Tessie died, even the youngest children who had known her sensed a sharp loss. Some felt guilty, said one teacher who met with them to talk about Tessie's life and to help them cope with her death. Perhaps, the teacher thought, as Tessie got older and a little forgetful, the children thought they might not have been sufficiently thoughtful and appreciative. A more plausible explanation may be that the children instinctively recognized an extraordinary teacher, and mourned the loss.[10]

Hortense Eugenie Tyroler taught English in the Middle School during Mrs. Durham's administration. She then went on to teach English electives in the High School during Donald Barr's and Gardner Dunnan's administrations. Her preparation included a B.A. from Vassar College and an M.A. from Columbia University. Her experience before coming to

---

[10] Fred M. Hechinger, "Gift of a Great Teacher," *The New York Times*, November 10, 1987.

Dalton was that of research assistant in American and English literature; writer and private tutor. "Miss T," as she was known to her students, was famous for her sharp mind, her witty responses, and her commitment to the philosophy of the school. Her courses, such as Russian Literature, Literary Criticism, and Journalism, were college-level courses, open to bold, brave, and venturesome Dalton high school students. "Miss T" retired in June, 1981. In October she addressed the Dalton faculty. The subject was "Words to the Faculty on the Dalton Plan." Her talk illustrates a lifelong commitment of a teacher to an independent experimental school eager to implement its philosophy, cognizant of the changes it must undergo, and still excited by the possibilities it offers:

> I am not one who believes that advanced age and wisdom are naturally concomitant—far from it—but some of us who have weathered Dalton storms—even hurricanes—for many decades do develop a kind of perspective on the activities of the school and of its students. Both Aaron and I have had a special interest in the Plan with a capital "P" which our founder explicated during her turbulent years with the Board of Trustees, the Parents and—may I add—the creditors.
>
> To believe that the Plan is sacrosanct would be sheer folly. There can never be a total "going back," a reversion to the "good old days" in a world that quite properly demands dynamic action. Any businessman will tell you that a firm which is satisfied to maintain the status quo will soon be subjected to diminishing returns.
>
> An increase in the population of the school, in the variety of courses offered, and in the number of new teachers bewildered by Dalton's often unspoken expectations must, perforce, develop administrative and academic techniques to meet the present situation. In trying to cope with today's problems, we have lost much that was effective years ago without replacement by equally operative methods. We would like to retain, however, the goals of the early school and to leave an inspired implementation up to you. The new addition to the report system, for example, is one such innovation calculated to reinforce the

bonds between a student and his teachers; and between the student and his House Advisor and to deepen the student's self-knowledge. The system requires time and tact but the dialogue involved is a learning process for all concerned and hopefully will succeed.

Leaving ourselves open to experimentation in all areas, we nevertheless should make a concerted effort to maintain Dalton ideals or, if you wish—to keep in mind our concerns.

What are these ideals?

The intellectual and emotional maturation of each student is our concern; the fulfillment of each student's potential is our concern; the development of each student's social conscience is our concern. These concerns sound like "pie in the sky" to cynics, but cynicism has never been a characteristic of the teaching profession. Relief in the amelioration of the human condition is fundamental to the educative process. Such a belief can be communicated to students only if there is a relationship between faculty and students which is based on mutual respect. Dalton's great success so far has been predicated on just such a kinship. We do not wish to lose this advantage.

Various schemes were tried to insure a steady progress toward the aforementioned goals. The three leading procedures included the role of the House Advisor, the time devoted to Laboratory, and the contractual Assignment. This afternoon I will recapitulate briefly some of the creative aspects of the last two contrivances: the Assignment and Lab, and then ask you to exert your resourcefulness in revitalizing The Plan.

Let us discuss the assignment first since Lab time depends on it to an important degree. The teacher has the opportunity to present in written form his or her pedagogic intentions for a stated period of time, making the subject matter of the course as attractive and as relevant as possible to the "party of the second part," the student who, in accepting the assignment, contracts to fulfill its directives to the best of his ability. The text should clarify the subject matter not only for the student but for the teacher himself as he considers various possible approaches before settling on the one he hopes will be successful. Creativity should not be the attribute solely of the student; a teacher's creativity is even more desirable.

Today's list of pages or exercises to be covered without any mention of the *raison d'etre* for covering them is sure to make Jack a dull boy. The introduction can and should be a preface worthy of reprinting and, most importantly, worthy of being read aloud to the class followed by free discussion. Any critical comments from the class members can be answered on the spot with reasonable explanations for the work to be covered, or adjustments can be made, if the teacher finds the comments helpful. Aristotle's "mean between the two extremes"—of ability in this case—should be central to the requirements, but opportunities for further investigation tangential to the core should also be incorporated for those who yearn for independent study projects. The Humanities have always been considered endearing but in today's world Science and Math are equally fascinating and can easily be related to a student's life outside of school.

Originally the contractual obligation was emphasized by progress reports. On a grid divided into four or more weeks for as many courses as the pupil was taking, the teacher's initials appeared at the end of each week, indicating that the expectations for that period of time had been satisfied, a silent message to the House Advisor that all was well. The advantage of such mundane bookkeeping was that no student could be found lacking points for graduation at the last moment. Steps were taken immediately to bring the laggard up to date.

Let us use the assignment to communicate our enthusiasm—not just for our own subject but for others as well. The connection with one or more disciplines can broaden the student's horizons by encouraging him to "make connections." Aaron Kurzen will speak further about this suggestion.

Now for Lab. The teacher in a one-to-one interview with a student or a group of four or five at a time has
a rich variety of options:
1. to explain in detail the why's of a paper's corrections,
2. to assist in the planning of a major paper,
3. to investigate further, concepts that have arisen during
class discussions,
4. to clarify meanings not always explained clearly in a
text, and
5. to guide the independent study projects offered in the
assignment.
These are the obvious values of Lab. The "secret
weapon" is the growth of mutual respect, dependent, of
course, on the attitudes of those involved.[11]

When Donald Barr became head of Dalton School, there was a mass
exodus of members of the old guard who had exercised an unusual amount
of autonomy during the Kittell administration. To preserve continuity, yet
mold in his own image, he hired recent graduates of Dalton, like myself, to
teach. He also hired young teachers of rigorous academic preparation and
"aristocratic birth" holding the same conservative political views as his own.
Two quintessential Barr teachers are a former director of Dalton's High
School, Dimitri Sevastopoulo, and a former teacher of Spanish, Gambino
Roche.

Dimitri Sevastopoulo came to Dalton in 1967 as a part-time teacher
of English. He was a Harvard graduate. His father, an aristocratic White
Russian, had fought in the Czar's army before emigrating to the West.
While at Dalton, Mr. Sevastopoulo completed his master's degree in
teaching at New York University. He then taught history, his major in
college, full-time in grades nine and ten during the academic year of
1968–69.

In the spring of 1969, the big moment arrived: Dimitri
Sevastopoulo was asked to become the Head of the High
School. He admitted that it was a surprise even though, as

---

[11]Gardner P. Dunnan, "Staff Memo," December 3, 1982.

with everything at Dalton, the news first came to him via rumor.[12]

Dimitri Sevastopoulo was at Dalton for a total of six years. He was an administrator for four of those years, during which time he appeared in custom-made suits and exercised his sense of noblesse oblige among students and faculty. He was admittedly a snob; he was admittedly inexperienced for the amount of responsibility that he was required to assume. Neither deficiency appeared to bother Barr. Dimitri Sevastopoulo possessed impeccable educational credentials and reflected a mode of conservatism in his outward appearance that made Barr feel comfortable. He helped set the tone Barr wished to project. And in the final analysis he proved to be a very decent person.

A second highly visible and unforgettable Barr teacher was a man by the name of Gabino Roche, a Cuban political refugee. "Señor" or The Roach—pun intended—as he was known to the student body, taught Spanish and, briefly, Latin American history. No documents exist regrading Señor's employment at Dalton; his academic preparation is unavailable to us. He vociferously shared his conservative ideas with students and faculty as a regular contributor to the High School paper, *The Daltonian*. His following letter to the editor sheds light on both Señor's political ideas and personal style:

I feel compelled to write this letter, due to the flagrant breach of confidence and total lack of seriousness and propriety exhibited by you.

Sometime ago several students and I decided that conservative political ideas should be presented before the faculty and student body at Dalton, as an alternative to the radical and irrational positions we believed to be unrepresentative of many a member of this academic community.

At first we thought about printing our own newspaper as a vehicle for the expression of the conservative position. However, the president of the student government and you approached me with the proposition that we join

---

[12]*The Daltonian*, November 19, 1970.

the *Daltonian*.

We agreed, on condition that the *Daltonian* would provide us with a column entitled *CONSERVATIVE VIEWPOINT*. You unreservedly agreed with our proposition, and consequently, the matter had apparently been resolved to the satisfaction of all concerned. You had indeed given your word and committed your personal integrity.

Nonetheless, our first article appeared in your issue of November 20th, but the title which was agreed upon by all of us for the column was left with the erroneous impression that said article was simply the doing of a single unrelated individual.

Unless there is a written and public retraction on your part, we will not submit additional articles, and as far as I am personally concerned, I will have nothing further to do with you or anyone connected with your publication.

I have no desire to be connected in any manner whatsoever with individuals who disregard honesty and moral integrity as mere bourgeois "hang-ups."[13]

Señor's physical appearance also belied his political ideology. Those who worked with him remember a short, stocky man always attired in a shirt, tie, and jacket, hair closely cropped in a "crew cut," sporting an American flag pin in his lapel. Señor did not walk down the halls; he strutted.

Señor's method of discipline was legendary. He would corner a student, "bark" accusations at him in an attempt to "break" him. His amateurish attempts at intimidation, resembling contemporary Cold War spy novel interrogation techniques, usually worked. Señor was both loud and persistent. He stood for law and order and would brook no nonsense—precisely the image Donald Barr might like to have been able to project, himself.

I have briefly discussed six teachers representing three administra-

---

[13]Ibid.

tions in Dalton's history. All had in common distinct personalities and, at some point in their lives, interest in their craft and commitment to the school. Of the six, four are deceased; one has left the profession for Wall Street; one remains unaccounted for. Each of them is unforgettable to those who were their students or colleagues.

*   *   *

Thus far I have argued that there are faculty members archetypical of the particular administrations from Parkhurst through Barr. While my categorization may work for these heads, it nevertheless breaks down in Gardner Dunnan's administration. Perhaps, as some informants suggest, this is due to the largeness of the organization; perhaps it is due to the differences in preferences of the headmaster and the associate headmaster. Gardner Dunnan, for example, seems to prefer credentials, either in education or subject matter while Frank Moretti, seeks teaching candidates who possess Ph.D's. Both in recent times, actively seek to employ minority candidates as well. There has been a trend to crossing over from to public to private sector, as in High School History Department Chair, Manny Harrison or former First Program Director, Stanley Seidman. There are also faculty (although seemingly fewer each year) who bridge a number of administrations: Alan Boyers, a physical education teacher who was hired by Charlotte Durham; Wayne Adamson, Middle School English teacher; Malcolm Thompson, High School science teacher; Sheila Lamb, First Program art teacher, Jan Barnett, First Program administrator, all hired by Donald Barr, and who continue to work at Dalton today. However, as the ranks of these individuals thin, collective memory of the past dims even more.

9

CONCLUSION: THE TRANSFORMATION OF A PROGRESSIVE SCHOOL

On May 6, 1988, the class of 1978 at the Dalton School had its ten-year reunion. There was a hard-rock singer from California, an investment banker who everyone had thought would go on to play the violin, doctors, lawyers, and numerous M.B.A.s. Notably absent were the class stars—Jennifer (*Dirty Dancing*) Grey and Tracy (*Family Ties*) Pollan, though Perri Peltz, a reporter for Channel 4 News, was there. Also absent were most of the Dalton students who had had serious problems with drugs...

By the end of the class' senior year both the world and Dalton were changing. Levis and flannel shirts yielded to Fioruccis at $50 a pop; dope and LSD yielded to Quaaludes and cocaine. Among parents the liberal and arts old guard was replaced by nouveau-riche and show-biz types because, whereas a photographer could no longer afford the $8000 or so tuition for the high school, an arbitrageur, for example, could. (One former teacher describes the current crop of parents at Dalton "who's who on new Wall Street.")[1]

Beginning with the Barr years, the Dalton School has received an unusual amount of publicity for an independent school. From such diverse sources as the *New York Times Magazine*, *New York Magazine*, *7 Days*, Woody Allen's *Manhattan*, and the more recent film with Diane Keaton, *Baby Boom*, Dalton has been in the public eye as a school where famous and affluent parents send their entitled offspring. From the character in *Baby Boom* bemoaning the end of her child's academic career after being rejected

---

[1]Fran Schumer, "Misplaced Generation—Dalton Class of '78," *7 Days*, January 4, 1989, pp. 29–30.

by Dalton's First Program, to Woody Allen's portrayal of a Dalton female adolescent as seventeen going on thirty, having an affair with a fortyish divorced male, to an advertisement stating "What do you say when Dalton accepts your toddler, Bloomingdale's Gold Card arrives for your wife, and your promotion just came through,"[2] to *7 Days'* muckraking attempt to sensationalize the drug problems of the Class of 1978, popular portrayals by the media have only provided part of the portrait. Indeed, the Dalton parent population, as I have previously indicated, has changed from one of artists, intellectuals, German Jews, and WASPS to, for the most part, one of high profile entertainers, artists, investment bankers, and real estate developers. What is missing here is the analysis of the transformation of the Dalton School from a small, experimental progressive school to a large, successful, competitive college preparatory school with a progressive tradition.

To briefly recapitulate the transformation of the school, the Dalton of Helen Parkhurst reflected the progressive movements of its time. It was often chaotic, disorganized, but at the same time it was an intimate, caring, nurturing, familial, and child-centered environment. It was also concerned with child growth and development, community and social service, and strove to effect a synthesis between the affective and cognitive domains of the child. Under Charlotte Durham, who inherited a financially troubled school, Dalton was able to retain its child-centered pedagogy, its caring and familial orientation, while at the same time placing more emphasis on academic rigor. It also was run in a more orderly and rational fashion and became perhaps less experimental and more legitimately a part of the New York City independent school world. In essence, Charlotte Durham's genius was to create a tradition out of its particular progressive experiment, with the Dalton Plan used as its guiding ritual. Under Donald Barr, the parent body began to change reflecting a higher proportion of the recently affluent, the curriculum and physical plant expanded, enrollment more than doubled, the High School became coeducational, and more emphasis was placed on academic rigor and achievement. As a result of all of this, conflict between faculty, students, parents, and administration inevitably erupted. In line with his antipathy for progressive education, which he equated with anti-intellectual and permissive miseducation, Barr began the transformation of Dalton into a large academically competitive institution. During a time of

---

[2]as quoted in the *Daltonian*, October 25, 1985.

social and political upheaval, in which adolescents were searching for individual meaning, Barr instituted strict disciplinary codes, often at odds with the cultural norms of the time and often impossible to enforce. He created a "hot" and desirable school, constantly in the public eye, and left it, like Helen Parkhurst, in financial and organizational disarray. Under Gardner Dunnan, who, like Charlotte Durham, inherited a school with serious problems, Dalton continued this transformation and became an organized, efficient, selective and academically rigorous institution. It eliminated its preschool, initiated an innovative learning disabilities program, and continued its expansion. That it is still a good school,[3] is unquestionable; that it is no longer a progressive school, in its progressive tradition, is the subject of the ensuing analysis.

*   *   *

From 1988 to 1991, a number of my graduate students conducting ethnographic research visited the Dalton School. Their research supports the conclusion of my own interviews, participant observation, and archival research that the school retains vestiges of its progressive tradition, that the rhetoric of the Dalton Plan is alive and used when convenient, but that on the whole Dalton represents a school that has compromised its particular progressive roots, perhaps as a consequence of the demands of a changing culture, and of a parent body far less concerned with educational theory and more concerned with status and academic success. The following description particularly suggests that Dalton has become an achievement oriented school:

> The emphasis at Dalton is clearly academic and achieve-
> ment oriented. The aim of the school is closely tied to the
> aim of the parents. This aim is shaped by the shared
> values, attitudes, and beliefs of the community the school
> serves. Thus there is a strong, positive ethos that drives the

---

[3]What constitutes a good school is a subject under considerable debate. For the purposes of this discussion see Sara Lawrence Lightfoot, *The Good High School* (New York: Basic Books, 1984).

school.

The curriculum is centered around a core set of subjects: math, science, English and history. Electives are available, but are in subjects like philosophy or modern politics; in other words, courses you might find in a good college. In each class I was impressed by level of discourse and the degree of engagement.

...I was interested to know if Dalton still subscribed to the progressive spirit of education. [An informant quite emphatically told me] that the school had changed completely. The emphasis was placed on achievement, and [that] the pressure to succeed had become the new identity of Dalton. Furthermore, this had occurred because the constituency that the school served demanded it to be so. In many ways the parents dictate the running of the school. Indeed during another discussion with a teacher, we were interrupted on numerous occasions by students with questions for the teacher. I was impressed by how the students had no qualms about interrupting the teacher and how the teacher did not hesitate to turn his attention from me immediately. In fact, the teacher stated quite frankly, that [teachers] must attend to the students immediately; it is expected.[4]

A former Dalton student, writing during her senior year echoes the theme of achievement both at Dalton and in the culture of the affluent upper middle class families who send their children to New York City independent schools:

In my house the use of the word college has been forbidden. It is simply classified as another one of the "four letter" words that my parents told me never to say in public. Much like the F-word or the S-word, in my house, the word college, has turned into the C-word. It is the only

---

[4]Peter Devlin, "In Search of a Stronger Positive Ethos," unpublished paper, December, 1991, pp. 8–9.

subject that will guarantee an immediate argument, make one member of the family burst into hysterics or send the entire family into group psychiatric care....

The C-word process can best be described in a list of five adjectives: Unpleasant, Unpleasant, Unpleasant, Nervewracking, and one of adjectives from the list of words your parents told you never to say in public. Once you enter that fated junior year, it all comes together. Parents and friends asking you that annoying question, "and WHERE do you want to go to college?" and your indecisive response, "I don't know." You are now branded a child without direction and if you haven't noticed already, these wise elders are telling you that this is the most important year in your entire life and you had better not mess (screw) it up.

There is no pressure involved in the C-word admissions process. Either you get into Harvard, or a school on par with the big H, get into Harvard graduate school, grow up and work for Goldman Sachs down on Wall Street (if it is still there) or if you don't, and become something else like a garbage collector....Although I have just entered the admissions process, people are already telling me that I have to get an A in Math so that I can get into Princeton.

With clenched jaws and haughty smiles most upper middle class private schoolers are walking around saying "I'm eastern establishment material, just look at my extracurricular activities: Varsity, Tennis 4 years, Editor of the *Daltonian*, frequent writer for the current events magazine *Macrocosm*, winner of 3 best delegate awards on the Harvard and Yale model U.N.'s, worked in a Soup Kitchen 189 hours,...father's income in the 8 digit range...," what is it all going to come down to? ...Although it is unavoidable, competition will strain friendships and everyone will feel alienated at one time or another. In the end it will be like Caesar's betrayal and Caesar (representing the alienated student) will be standing there saying to all the traitors "Et tu Brute, et tu." In the end, everybody gets in some-

> where and all past disagreements are resolved. It is then
> that people realize that college is not the end all and be all,
> Black Monday [the day Ivy League colleges send out their
> acceptance letters] is not judgement day and college is not
> the end of one's life; it is the beginning.[5]

As I indicated in the preceding chapter, recent evaluations of the
Dalton School, including those by NYSAIS, suggest that the Dalton Plan,
an important representation of its progressive tradition, is alive, but not
necessarily well. Although House, Lab, and Assignment exist, they no
longer serve as the linchpin of the school and they are implemented
inconsistently, without a clear focus. The school has become more
concerned with academic rigor and excellence, perhaps reflecting parental
concern with ensuring that their children will be admitted to Ivy League
colleges. There are to be sure efforts to revive its progressive tradition, for
example, the philosophy course introduced in the High School dealing with
progressive philosophy, and a committee effort led by Frank Moretti
culminating in a working paper, "Assignment on the Assignment," which
attempted to revitalize the creative use of the Assignment.

The ethos of achievement and competition is troubling to many who
remember the Dalton of the past. One student, writing in 1984, commented
that "Perhaps I should just accept the fact that Dalton is no longer guided
by the words of Helen Parkhurst and that when we now use the term Dalton
Plan, we refer to whatever philosophy the administration is presently
purveying."[6] Another commenting on the change in the school's ambience
during his fifteen years at Dalton (N–12) stated:

> ...The Dalton Plan is supposed to be student and teacher
> working together, developing a relationship, and maybe
> even being friends. What has happened to Dalton in these
> past fifteen years? When I was in eighth grade, I was
> friendly with almost all of my teachers. I would go to them
> with problems, and they would help me. Now that simply
> isn't true. With the exception of a few and, of course, my

---

[5]Meredith Fiedler, "College—The C-Word," The Dalton School, 1988.
[6]*The Daltonian*, March 1, 1984.

friends, I feel alone at Dalton. I feel it is me against them. Maybe this isn't true for everyone, but it is for me and I felt I had to say something.[7]

Finally, a former student running for alumni representative to the Board of Trustees had this to say:

> I believe in a Dalton School devoted not so much to the current religion of educational excellence as to a determination to provide an individualized educational program to each child no matter what the nature of his or her gifts. This kind of openness to the varying needs and abilities of each child was the essence of the Dalton Plan as I knew it. I also believe in a Dalton School that is focused on teaching children to think and communicate those thoughts to others; that is, committed to giving children the courage to follow their consciences.
>
> ...One of the things that most concerns me about Dalton today is the policy of weeding out kids who can't do "Dalton work." With the resources Dalton has we should have the ability and the commitment to educate every child. If a child cannot be educated at Dalton where can he or she be educated?"[8]

Although some might disagree with the notion that a school such as Dalton has an obligation to educate all children, even if they are not able to handle the level of work, this statement clearly indicates how far Dalton has strayed from the original intent of the Dalton Plan, reflecting the ideas of Parkhurst, Dewey, and Montessori, that a school could do exactly this. Given the fact that Dalton is now more than triple its original size, it may be far more difficult to do this. Nonetheless, the consistent theme of many veteran Dalton teachers and former students reflects a sense of loss for the particular type of child-centered pedagogy the school once represented.

That the Dalton School is a distinctly different school today is clear.

---

[7]*The Daltonian*, June 8, 1983.
[8]Letter to Dalton Alumnae/i, The Dalton School, August 15, 1991.

Whether such change was necessary and inevitable is a difficult and complex issue. In order to analyze this question one must examine a multitude of historical, organizational, and sociological factors affecting school change, including the history of educational reform, changes in the culture, and independent school leadership. Although no single one explains the changes at the Dalton School, nevertheless, as I will argue, leadership by the school head emerges as a significant, if not dominant element.

*   *   *

On the one hand, to understand the transformation of a school such as Dalton, its changes must be placed in the larger context of the history of educational reforms. On the other hand, as an independent school, Dalton was far more insulated than public schools from state mandates and the need to respond to political agendas outside of its parent body. Nevertheless, the external social and political conditions certainly affected Dalton, if only to serve as a mirror in which to view itself. Recent criticisms of public education, such as Chubb and Moe's *Politics, Markets, and Schools* suggest that the bureaucratic nature of public education is at odds with school improvement and that privatization is part of the remedy to educational problems. Although clearly schools such as Dalton have far more autonomy than public schools, it is not my intention to enter this debate here. Nor should this statement be used to support their thesis; it is far too complicated and not germane to this discussion.[9]

In the introduction, I demonstrated how the Dalton School under Helen Parkhurst reflected the progressive movement of the early twentieth century. Influenced by Dewey, Montessori, and Washburne, Parkhurst founded a child-centered, progressive institution. The Dalton School, like its progressive counterparts, City and Country, Walden, Lincoln, and Bank Street, represented Deweyan principles in a variety of interpretations. In the ensuing years, each one responded to the changing times in a different way. Some, such as Walden and Lincoln, ultimately closed their doors; others such as City and Country and Bank Street, have retained a good deal of

---

[9]see *Teachers College Record*, Fall, 1991, for a complete discussion of the debate over Chubb and Moe's book.

their progressive traditions as they struggle to remain financially solvent; and Dalton, the most financially successful and stable of the lot, has retained the least visible evidence of its progressive legacy. To help understand this phenomenon it is necessary to trace briefly the history of educational reform beginning with the reaction against progressive education.[10] For Dalton, this begins during the Durham administration in the 1940's.

In the 1940's many of the patterns that emerged during the Progressive Era were continued. First, the debate about the goals of education (i.e., academic, social, or both) and whether all children should receive the same education remained an important one. Second, the demand for the expansion of educational opportunity became perhaps the most prominent feature of educational reform. Particularly, the post-World War II years were concerned with expanding opportunities to the post-secondary level. They were also directed at finding ways to translate these expanded opportunities into more equal educational outcomes at all levels of education. As in the first half of the 20th century, so too, in the second half, the compatibility of expanded educational opportunity with the maintenance of educational standards would create serious problems. Thus, the tensions between equity and excellence became crucial in the debates of this period. Ultimately, the expansion of post-secondary education resulted in a credential expansion making not only a college education necessary, but more importantly, where one went to college. For schools like Dalton, this post-World War II credential inflation resulted in a far greater emphasis on college admissions than ever before. Concurrently, as very selective colleges placed more emphasis on grades and SAT scores as the basis for admission, Dalton responded in kind.

The post-World War II years witnessed the continuation of the processes that defined the development of the comprehensive high school. The debates over academic issues, which began at the turn of the century, may be defined as the movement between pedagogical progressivism and pedagogical traditionalism. This is a pattern that originated at the turn of the

---

[10]The following section on the history of education is adapted from Susan F. Semel, Peter W. Cookson, Jr. and Alan R. Sadovnik, "Educational Reform in the United States" in Peter W. Cookson, Jr., Alan R. Sadovnik and Susan F. Semel, *International Handbook of Educational Reform* (Westport, CT: Greenwood Press, 1992), Chapter 25.

century and one that has focused not only on the process of education but on its goals. At the center of these debates are the questions regarding the type of education children should receive and whether all children should receive the same education. While many of these debates were over curriculum and method, they ultimately were associated with the question of equity versus excellence. Perhaps these debates can be best understood by examining reform cycles of the 20th century which revolved between progressive and traditional visions of schooling. On the one hand, traditionalists believed in knowledge centered education, a traditional subject centered curriculum, teacher-centered education, discipline and authority, and the defense of academic standards in the name of excellence. On the other hand, progressives believed in experiential education, a curriculum that responded to both the needs of students and the times, child centered education, freedom and individualism, and the relativism of academic standards in the name of equity. While these are poles and educational practices rarely reflected one direction, the conflicts over educational policies and practices seemed to move back and forth between these two extremes. From 1945–1955, the progressive education of the previous decades was critically attacked.

These critics, including Mortimer Smith, Robert Hutchins, and Arthur Bestor assailed progressive education for its sacrificing of intellectual goals to social ones. They argued that the life adjustment education of the period combined with an increasingly anti-intellectual curriculum destroyed the traditional academic functions of schooling. Arthur Bestor, a respected historian and a classmate, interestingly enough of Donald Barr's at the Lincoln School, argued that it was "regressive education" not progressive education that had eliminated the school's primary role in teaching children to think.[11] Bestor, like the other critics, assailed the schools for destroying the democratic vision that all students should receive an education that was once reserved for the elite and suggested that the social and vocational emphasis of the schools indicated a belief that all students could not learn academic material. In an ironic sense, many of the conservative critics were agreeing with the radical critique that the Progressive Era distorted the ideals of democratic education by tracking poor and working class children

---

[11]Diane Ravitch, *The Troubled Crusade* (New York: Basic Books, 1983), p. 76.

into non-academic vocational programs.

Throughout the 1950s the debate between progressives who defended the social basis of the curriculum and critics who demanded a more academic curriculum raged on. What was often referred to as "the great debate"[12] ended with the Soviets launching of the space satellite Sputnik. The idea that the Soviets would win the race for space resulted in a national commitment to improve educational standards in general and to increase mathematical and scientific literacy, in particular. From 1957 through the mid 1960's the emphasis shifted to the pursuit of excellence and curriculum reformers attempted to redesign the curricula in ways that would lead to the return of academic standards (although many doubted that such a romantic age ever existed).

During the Durham years, when these criticisms of progressive education were rampant, Dalton did not cave in to popular demands for change. Although Durham built upon the already existing academic tradition and strengthened it, she never abandoned the Dalton Plan. Perhaps this was possible because there was considerable agreement among faculty and parents that what Dalton represented was valuable and worth preserving. Within this culture, Durham was able to use its progressive tradition as the glue with which to hold the school together.

By the mid 1960s, however, the shift in educational priorities moved again toward the progressive side. This occurred in two distinct but overlapping ways. First, the Civil Rights movement, lead to an emphasis on equity issues. Thus, federal legislation, such as the Elementary and Secondary Education Act of 1965, emphasized the education of disadvantaged children. Second, in the context of the antiwar movement of the times, the general criticism of American society, and the persistent failure of the schools to ameliorate problems of poverty and of racial minorities, a "new progressivism" developed that linked the failure of the schools to the problems in society. Ushered in by the publication of A.S. Neill's *Summerhill* in 1960, a book about an English boarding school with few, if any rules and which was dedicated to the happiness of the child, the new progressivism provided an intellectual and pedagogical assault on the putative sins of traditional education, its authoritarianism, its racism, its misplaced values of intellectualism, and its failure to meet the emotional and psychological

---

[12]Ibid., p.79.

needs of children.

Throughout the 1960s and early 1970s a variety of books provided scathing criticism of American education including Jonathan Kozol's *Death at an Early Age*, which assailed the racist practices of the Boston public schools; Herbert Kohl's *36 Children*, demonstrated the pedagogical possibilities of "open education"; and Charles S. Silberman's *Crisis in the Classroom* attacked the bureaucratic, stultifying mindlessness of American education. These books, along with a series of articles by Joseph Featherstone and Beatrice and Ronald Gross on British progressive or open education[13] resulted in significant experimentation in some American schools. Emphasis on individualism and relevant education, along with the challenge to the unquestioned authority of the teacher, resulted in "alternative," "free," or "open" education: schooling that once again shifted attention away from knowledge (product) to process. Although there is little evidence to suggest that the open classroom was a national phenomenon, and as the historian Larry Cuban notes in his history of teaching, *How Teachers Taught*, there has been surprisingly little variation in the 20th century in teacher methods (that is, despite the cycles of debate and reform, most secondary teachers still lecture more than they involve students), the period from the mid 1960s to the mid-1970s was a time of great turmoil in the educational arena: a time marked by two simultaneous processes. The first, the challenge to traditional schooling and the second, the attempt to provide educational opportunity for the disadvantaged.

Just as the educational reform pendulum swung back to a more progressive side,[14] Dalton began to echo the cries of Arthur Bestor and

---

[13]Joseph Featherstone's articles in the *New Republic* are in *Schools Where Children Learn* (New York: Liveright, 1971); Beatrice and Ronald Gross, "A Little Bit of Chaos," *Saturday Review*, May 16, 1970.

[14]There is some disagreement among historians of education about the progressivism of this period. On the one hand, Diane Ravitch argues in *The Troubled Crusade*, Chapter 7, that these reforms were examples of "romantic progressivism" of the type Dewey criticized in *Experience and Education* (New York: Macmillan, 1938) as too extreme in their emphasis on freedom. On the other hand, Larry Cuban, in *How Teachers Taught*, argues that these reforms were not progressive in the historical sense. He calls it "informal education," thus distinguishing it from progressive

the other conservative critics. In hiring Donald Barr, the school may not have known precisely what it was getting. In fact, one informant recalls Barr explicitly stating that "When I came in in 1963 I had my butch hair cut and my American flag. They didn't know what they hired. I am a reactionary and proud of it." The informant continued that Barr was in fact surprised that they had hired him. In attempting to keep the 1960s at bay, Barr instituted dress codes, haircut regulations, and anti-drug policies. Although this, not surprisingly, garnered him significant parental support, especially among the new Dalton parents, it alienated the old Daltonians, who equated Dalton with individual freedom and expression. Further, it alienated a significant portion of the student body.

In line with the reforms that would come after his resignation, Barr sought to infuse greater academic rigor into the curriculum. In line with the demands of a changing parent body and a culture in which credential inflation had now become ascendent,[15] Barr turned Dalton into a school with, in his own words, "pizazz."

By the late 1970s, conservative critics again began to react to the educational reforms of the 1960s and 1970s. They argued that liberal reforms in pedagogy and curriculum and in the arena of educational opportunity had resulted in the decline of authority and standards. Furthermore, they stated that the preoccupation with using the schools to ameliorate social problems, however well intended, not only failed to do this, but was part of an overall process that resulted in mass mediocrity. What was needed, was nothing less than a complete overhaul of the American educational system. While radical critics also pointed to the failure of the schools to ameliorate problems of poverty, they located the problem not so much in the schools, but in the society at large. Liberals defended the reforms of the period by suggesting that social improvement takes a long time, and a decade and a half was scarcely sufficient to turn things around.

In 1983, the National Commission on Excellence, founded by President Reagan's Secretary of Education, Terrence Bell, issued its now famous report, *A Nation at Risk*. This report provided a serious indictment

---

education.

[15]For a detailed discussion of the history and sociology of credentialism, see Randall Collins, *The Credential Society* (New York: Academic Press, 1979).

of American education and cited high rates of adult illiteracy, declining SAT scores, and low scores on international comparisons of knowledge by American students as examples of the decline of literacy and standards. The Committee stated that "the educational foundations of our society are presently being eroded by a rising tide of mediocrity that threatens our very future as a Nation and a people."[16] As solutions, the Commission offered five recommendations: (1) that all students graduating from high school complete what was termed the "new basics"—four years of English, three years of mathematics, three years of science, three years of social studies, and a half year of computer science; (2) that schools at all levels expect higher achievement from their students and that 4 year colleges and universities raise their admissions requirements; (3) that more time be devoted to teaching the new basics; (4) that the preparation of teachers be strengthened and that teaching be made a more respected and rewarded profession; (5) that citizens require their elected representatives to support and fund these reforms.[17]

The years following this report were characterized by scores of other reports that both supported the criticism and called for reform. During the 1980's significant attention was given to the improvement of curriculum, the tightening of standards, and the move to the setting of academic goals and their assessment. A coalition of American governors took on a leading role in setting a reform agenda; business leaders stressed the need to improve the nation's schools and proposed partnership programs; the federal government, through its Secretary of Education (under Ronald Reagan) William Bennett, took an active and critical role, but continued to argue that it was not the federal government's role to fund such reform; and educators, at all levels, struggled to have a say in determining the nature of the reforms.

The politics of the reform movement were complex and multidimensional. Conservatives wanted to restore both standards and the traditional curriculum; liberals demanded that the new drive for excellence not ignore

---

[16]U.S. Commission on Excellence in Education, *A Nation at Risk* (Washington D.C.: Government Printing Office, 1983), p. 5.

[17]Lawrence A. Cremin, *Popular Education and its Discontents* (New York: Harper and Row, 1990), p. 31.

the goals for equity; radicals believed it was another pendulum swing doomed to failure and one that sought to reestablish excellence as a code word for elitism.

Gardner Dunnan arrived at Dalton in 1975 at the tail end of the progressive revival and the beginning of the conservative reaction. Dunnan himself admits that his original plan was to go back to the Dalton Plan and to "try and link what we do to the philosophy and heritage of the school."[18] He also believes "that we have moved to a closer approximation of the Dalton Plan today than when I arrived fifteen years ago."[19] Although this may well be true in comparison to the school left to him by Donald Barr, it is nonetheless far less progressive than it once was. It is more the case that the Dalton School, under Dunnan, reflects the concerns of the culture and the educational reform movements of the 1980s more than it reflected the concerns of the 1960s and 1970s under Donald Barr. With its emphasis on academic excellence, on technology, on accountability and efficiency, on the use of common examinations and common assignments, Dalton has lost much of the emphasis on the individual child learning at his or her own pace (with the exception of the Fisher-Landau Program) and often seems more in line with the effective school movement[20] than the progressive movement.

During both the Barr and Dunnan years there has been some response to the other feature of the post-World War II period, namely the quest for equality of opportunity. This continues the strong tradition of the school to improve society. There has been a considerable attempt to increase scholarship monies for students whose parents cannot afford the tuition and, in particular, efforts under Dunnan to recruit minority students. In fact, in his Annual Report of 1989, titled "Diversity and Excellence," Dunnan points to his accomplishments in this area. Also, the Long Range Plan includes as a goal increased minority enrollment in order to increase diversity. To suggest that a selective school such as Dalton plays any role in reducing inequalities of educational opportunity may seem oxymoronic to some. However, in keeping with the tradition of providing opportunities for

---

[18]Interview with Gardner P. Dunnan, December 8, 1990.

[19]Ibid.

[20]For a discussion of this movement, see Cookson Jr, Sadovnik, and Semel, Chapter 25.

students who would otherwise be unable to attend, Dalton has continued to play a small role in addressing equity issues.

This brief historical analysis suggests that Dalton, to some degree, mirrored the reforms of the last fifty years. The school is certainly more traditional today than it was in Helen Parkhurst's time. It does not, however, parallel these reforms directly. As I have demonstrated, Charlotte Durham and Donald Barr were far more resistant to the temper of the times than Helen Parkhurst and Gardner Dunnan. What this suggests is that leadership and the personality of the school head are important factors in explaining how Dalton changed.

* * *

In the introduction to my history of the Dalton School I stated that the principle of this study was that the head of the school plays a very significant role in making the school what it is. My research supports the thesis that the head of the school is instrumental in determining its course, in establishing its tone, neighborhood and contemporary concerns notwithstanding. This is in part due to Dalton's internal structure, a structure in which the only constant is the head of the school.

In very different contexts, Roland Barth[21] and Seymour Sarason concur. Sarason states that "the principal is the crucial implementor of change. That is to say, any proposal for change that intends to alter the quality of life in the school depends primarily on the principal."[22] And for the head of an independent school to be successful he or she must create a regime; a support system that will enable that school head to formulate and implement school policy. All of Dalton's heads have in fact done this, save Jack Kittell; Helen Parkhurst, Charlotte Durham, Donald Barr, and Gardner Dunnan formed social relationships which enabled them to influence individuals or groups of individuals. Each in turn created a regime based on personal loyalties and, in some cases, the feudal-like principle of reciprocity. Whether or not the school head will be moved to action, however,

---

[21]See, Barth, *Run School Run*.

[22]Seymour Sarason, *The Culture of the School and the Problem of Change* (Boston: Allyn and Bacon, 1971), p. 148.

depends upon "the principal's conception of himself in relation to the system."[23]

Maxine Greene articulates another perspective on this subject that may prove useful to readers:

> A great deal depends on how the teacher[24] adjusts his perspectives on human beings and the institutions they have made. Much also depends on how he chooses himself as a teacher, how he decides to act on what he has come to know.[25]

Four of the heads of Dalton, in particular, saw "possibilities" and chose to work "authentically toward the realization of possibilities."[26] And in turn, each molded the school in his or her own image.

The first, Helen Parkhurst, created Dalton, improvising as she went along. In her colleague Elizabeth Seeger's words, there was an "exhilaration" and "recklessness" that characterized the school's early years; I might have used the same adjectives to characterize Helen Parkhurst, herself. For Parkhurst, implemented and publicized a particular educational philosophy that was, at best, a synthesis of current educational ideas of her contemporaries. She created a school in bold, broad strokes, with the aid of wealthy patrons such as Mrs. W. Murray Crane. She duplicated her efforts in such then remote places as Chile and Japan. She made Dalton a desirable school for children to attend. But Helen Parkhurst was a poor administrator and a poor financial manager. In the end, her chaotic administration collapsed under the weight of bankruptcy.

Charlotte Durham, her successor and former assistant, stabilized Dalton and brought to it an air of respectability. Under her leadership and with the able assistance of Stanley M. Isaacs, the school became financially solvent. It also became an experimental school in educational philosophy only; its tone, like Charlotte Durham, was decidedly formal and rational.

---

[23]Ibid.

[24]Read principal.

[25]Maxine Greene, *Teacher as Stranger* (Belmont, Calif.: Wadsworth Publishing Co., 1973), p. 65.

[26]Ibid., p. 62.

Dalton was brought into the world of the "guild" schools; college admissions became significant; thus, a note of academic rigor was duly injected into the High School. Conferences were regularized, examinations in certain courses were given; even grades were presented to each high school student at the close of the eleventh year. The atmosphere on the second floor, home of the administration, was "hushed." Few students and fewer parents ventured down the corridor, save if they were summoned.

The third head to seize upon the possibilities afforded by Dalton and to mold the school in his image was Donald Barr. Utilizing the same bold strokes as Helen Parkhurst, he cajoled money from wealthy patrons and publicized Dalton through the media, making it a desirable school to send one's children to. In his tenure as headmaster, Donald Barr increased the school's size by 300 percent. He acquired additional instructional and physical education facilities, created academic departments, instituted an elective program, and introduced boys in the High School.

Like Parkhurst, Barr was a publicist; and like Parkhurst, Barr had an educational philosophy. But unlike Parkhurst, Barr was a conservative "back to basics" proponent. Donald Barr was by far the most creative thinker and the most articulate speaker of the first three principal heads. But he, too, like Dalton's founder, was a poor administrator and financial manager. He had difficulty delegating responsibility to competent administrators; he often chose weak middle level managers and thus had to play the role of the deus ex machina. On a daily basis, Barr's administration had the same frenzied quality; the same exhilaration and recklessness that characterized Dalton's early years. In the end, rapid expansion and its accompanying economic problems, as well as conflicts with teachers, parents, and students forced Barr's resignation. Yet the personality of the head of an independent school looms large in its destiny. "Conditions" are important factors in determining the course a school will take; leadership of the head is another. In Barr's case, particularly, I believe that he attracted many parents who wished to remove their children from "the temper of the times." That he had difficulty doing this was another matter.

In 1975, after a brief period under an interim head, Gardner Dunnan became headmaster of Dalton. Like Charlotte Durham who followed the nonrational administration of her predecessor, Gardner Dunnan inherited a school in chaos and brought it order. He balanced the budget, created a published pay scale for faculty, set procedures for channels of communication and decision-making, and acquired another building for instructional purposes at the First Program. From the outset, the situation he inherited forced him to act in the mode of what Seymour Sarason would term an "educational administrator." This in itself is not a pejorative term; it is simply that Dalton was a school requiring of a head the ability to put its house in order.

Once Gardner Dunnan stabilized the school, he then had the opportunity to put his own mark on Dalton as the educational leader of a school rife with possibilities and rich in tradition. Of the four school heads, Gardner Dunnan is clearly the best professional manager. Unlike his predecessors, he brought systematic planning to the operation of the school. He also established a rational-bureaucratic structure, which ensured the smooth everyday running of the school. That this structure often was in opposition to the more spontaneous aspects of progressive practice frequently upset longtime members of the Dalton community; that it may have saved a school in financial turmoil is unquestionable.

To what degree the school needed to continue its transformation from progressivism to its current more traditional emphasis is unclear. Could Gardner Dunnan have moved, as he originally says he intended, back to Dalton's progressive roots? On the one hand, Donald Barr's conservativism, in the face of radical upheaval and turbulent times, suggests that the school head can swim upstream against the tide of educational and cultural norms. On the other hand, Gardner Dunnan went in the opposite direction, choosing to move the school more closely in line with the concerns of the times. Perhaps because Gardner Dunnan does not lead through the cult of personality, as did Parkhurst and Barr, he may have found it more difficult to move against the tide. Additionally, Dunnan has the least articulated, consistent philosophy of education and thus the school under his leadership came to reflect his managerial style rather than his particular philosophical viewpoint. Some suggest that it was precisely this characteristic that led Dunnan to hire Frank Moretti, as Dalton's "philosopher king."

This discussion of leadership at the Dalton School supports sociologist Max Weber's typology of leadership and authority.[27] Weber distinguished three ideal types of authority: charismatic, traditional, and rational-legal. The first, based on the cult of personality, is inherently

---

[27]Hans Gerth and C. Wright Mills, *From Max Weber: Essays in Sociology* (New York: Oxford University Press, 1946), pp. 196–266.

unstable, as once the leader leaves or dies, there is rarely another charismatic leader waiting in the wings, both because charisma is a scarce resource and charismatic leaders rarely hire other charismatic individuals for fear that they will eclipse them. The second, based upon the adherence to tradition, is used by leaders to create stability within an organization. Often, as in the Roman Catholic Church, when a charismatic leader dies, as with Christ, subsequent authority is based upon creating a tradition out of the original leader's teachings, which become ritual and gospel. The third, which Weber associated with the modern bureaucratic state, is based on formal, systematic, and rational rules.

The leadership of the four school heads at Dalton personifies these categories. Helen Parkhurst was a charismatic leader, whose regime waxed and waned in relation to the vicissitudes of her personality. Upon her removal, the school needed stability and Charlotte Durham provided it. She was a traditional leader, who created allegiance to the teachings of Helen Parkhurst and turned the progressive philosophy of its founder into ritual. Her principal successor, Donald Barr, like Helen Parkhurst, was a charismatic leader, and like her, molded the school in his own image, created controversy, and left it in chaos. Finally, its present head, Gardner Dunnan, like Charlotte Durham, had to save a school in financial and organizational difficulty. Unlike Durham, he did not turn to the school's progressive tradition, but rather instituted a rational-legal structure to return it to stability. Perhaps because of his public school administrative background, where such a bureaucratic style is a matter of course, or perhaps as a consequence of his personal preference, Dunnan steered the school on its present, more organized, more traditional, more stable, direction.

What does the history of the Dalton School tell us about the factors affecting school change? The Dalton School changed with the times, reflecting to some degree the educational reforms of the last fifty years. It changed also as its parent body changed, reflecting more fully their concerns for their children's futures, concerns parents during the Parkhurst and Durham eras did not, on the whole, possess.[28] Most importantly, it

---

[28] It is not that parents in the Parkhurst and Durham eras were less concerned about their children's futures, but that in these periods affluent parents could more easily pass on their class advantages to their children, without their children necessarily obtaining an Ivy League education. In

changed as a result of the leadership and personality of its school heads, each of which put his or her indelible stamp on the school. Whether or not the Dalton School could have remained more progressive and still survived is not a question that can be answered here. What is clear is that it is a school transformed from the one founded by Helen Parkhurst. It is also a different world.

---

these times, prior to the rise of rampant credentialism, Dalton parents were less concerned with what a Dalton education would "buy" their offspring in terms of future educational choices. Moreover, prior to the mass expansion of post-secondary education, Dalton parents were perhaps more secure of their ability to secure their children's futures.

EPILOGUE

THE DALTON SCHOOL AND PROGRESSIVE EDUCATION

This history of the Dalton School traced the transformation of an independent progressive school, from its early experimental roots in the Deweyan tradition, to a more traditional, highly competitive, elite college preparatory school today. Although the school still maintains vestiges of its progressive heritage, it is, nevertheless, a very different school than the one Helen Parkhurst founded. As I concluded in the previous chapter, given the dramatic changes over the past 73 years both in education and in society, it is not at all surprising that such change did occur. The question is, however, to what extent did the school need to change in the more traditional direction that it took. Would it have been possible for it to have remained more faithful to the vision of its founder or did the social, economic, political, and cultural demands placed upon it mandate its transformation?

It is important to note that in order to answer adequately such important historical and policy questions about progressive education, we need more than one case study. This history of the Dalton School, by itself, cannot form the basis for definitively answering questions concerning the decline or maintenance of historical progressive traditions. Indeed, other independent progressive schools, founded during the same period, have chosen different paths. Some, including City and Country School, have remained faithful to their founders' vision and today the school is a far more child-centered and democratic community than Dalton. It is also far more cognizant of the traditions of its founder, Caroline Pratt, than Dalton is of Helen Parkhurt. Others, such as the Walden School and the Lincoln School are now defunct, as they failed to accommodate successfully to the demands of the market and the changing educational times. To be fair, City and Country is struggling financially and Dalton is in far better financial shape. Additionally, because City and Country only goes through grade eight, it has been more insulated from the demands of parents concerning college admissions. Finally, City and Country is a much smaller school. It is apparent that to address properly these questions, a comparative historical approach is necessary, one that this book cannot provide. Nonetheless, the history of the Dalton School provides important data for such comparative historical research.

Writing in the 1990s, one is encouraged by the increased interest in progressive education. After over a decade of conservative domination of educational discourse, and during a period where school choice, tuition vouchers, and wide-spread loss of faith in public education are the foundation for George Bush's educational initiative *America 2000*, it is heartening to see educators who are looking instead to more progressive models. For example, in May 1992, at a two day conference of educators sponsored by the National Center for Restructuring Education, Schools and Teaching (NCREST) at Teachers College, Columbia University, time and again educators echoed the need to restructure schools along the line of the democratic and egalitarian community envisioned by Dewey almost a century earlier. There was a stark contrast between the rhetoric of Washington based reform with its emphasis on assessment, accountability, and excellence and the conference's concern with progressive principles and practices such as equity, democracy, integrated curriculum, authentic assessment, and cooperative learning.

It was somewhat ironic that some conference participants had little awareness of the historical roots of the practices that they advocated. That this conference was aimed primarily at public school educators and that the majority of the sessions dealt with public schools, raises two important issues. First, in the 1920s and 1930s many progressive experiments were generated in the private sector. Progressive education in the public schools were more often than not a distorted version of Deweyanism, representing the triumph of what historian David Tyack has termed administrative progressivism. In the 1990s, when interest in progressive education comes from educators in the public schools as well as the private schools, many of the progressive practices supported by public educators have their origins in independent progressive schools like Dalton. Second, the overwhelming concern with equity expressed by public educators raises a significant issue concerning progressive education at a school such as Dalton. That is, can a school that from its inception catered to an economically elite population (scholarships not withstanding), really be taken seriously as a progressive school? As I noted in Chapter 1, Deweyan progressive education by the 1920s more often than not was found in independent schools, such as Dalton. That their populations were often composed of children of the affluent upper middle classes, while posing a political problem for progressives, is nonetheless a reality. Thus, any discussion of the history of the Dalton School as a progressive school must take into account this progressive paradox. Can a school that educates affluent children, however artsy and intellectual their parents, truly educate for democracy? This is a question that Dalton has long grappled with, witness the concern for minority student representation at Dalton from Charlotte Durham to Gardner Dunnan. What this paradox indicates is that a discussion of Dalton and progressive education must recognize that Dalton is not, and never was, a public school. It must be examined for what it is, an independent school with a progressive tradition. Contemporary concerns with equity, although exceedingly important, should not be used to render the discussion invalid. Despite the paradox, the history of Dalton provides much insight about progressive education.

This history of the Dalton School has argued that the school has significantly strayed from its original progressive roots. The question remains, to what extent, then, is the Dalton School today a progressive school? Using the statement of principles of the steering committee of the Network of Progressive Educators drafted on November 10, 1990, the following section will examine the degree to which Dalton reflects a number of progressive principles.[1] According to the Network's statement:

Fundamental principles and assumptions include:

---

[1] It is important to note that such use of contemporary principles is historically problematic in judging the history of a school, as they impose a contemporary view of progressive education, which may not be appropriate for a given period in the school's history. Thus, while it is used to examine the school's history, as well as its current status as a progressive school, it is important to note the limitations of these contemporary definitions of progressive education. Second, as they are written to include both the public and private sectors, and may indeed reflect an emphasis on public education, some of the principles may not easily apply to the Dalton School, especially those related to diverse cultures. Nonetheless, as a heuristic device it is helpful in providing a framework for understanding the transformation of the Dalton School.

● Education is best accomplished where relationships are personal and teachers design programs which honor the linguistic and cultural diversity of the local community.

● Teachers, as respected professionals, are crucial sources of knowledge about teaching and learning.

● Curriculum balance is maintained by commitment to children's individual interests and developmental needs, as well as a commitment to community within and beyond the school's walls.

● Schools embrace the home cultures of children and their families. Classroom practices reflect these values and bring multiple cultural perspectives to bear.

● Students are active constructors of knowledge and learn through direct experience and primary sources.

● All disciplines—the arts, sciences, humanities, and physical development—are valued equally in an interdisciplinary curriculum.

● Decision making within schools is inclusive of children, parents, and staff.

● The school is a model of democracy and humane relationships confronting issues of racism, classism, and sexism.

● Schools actively support critical inquiry into the complexities of global issues. Children can thus assume the powerful responsibilities of world citizenship.[2]

---

[2]Network of Progressive Educators, "Statement of Principles", *Pathways*, Vol. 7, Number 2 (February, 1991), p.3.

Although clearly a document reflecting a 1990s progressive agenda in language, it is a useful synthesis of historically progressive and reconstructionist notions about the role of progressive schools in society. How, then, does the Dalton School fare when examined against these principles?

- Education is best accomplished where relationships are personal and teachers design programs which honor the linguistic and cultural diversity of the local community:

Although some students suggest that Dalton has become too large and impersonal, there remains a philosophical commitment to personal relationships through House and Lab, although both have been criticized by both students and faculty, as well as external evaluators for not performing their original functions. Personal relationships were always a hallmark of Dalton, especially during the Parkhurst and Durham administrations. As the school increased in size under Barr and Dunnan, and became more rational and bureaucratic under the latter, the intimacy has declined. To say that the school is impersonal would be untrue; it is just less familial than it was in the past.

In terms of honoring the linguistic and cultural diversity of the local community, this is one of the principles ill suited to the Dalton School. It does mirror its local community. The problem is that the community is not truly diverse. To be fair, the Dalton School has attempted to create a more diverse and multicultural population, but as I have suggested this has been less successful in the lower grades where children must rely on their parents for transportation to school. As an independent school with a high tuition, even with significant scholarship aid, the school cannot mirror the diversity of society at large. As I mentioned above, if this disqualifies such a school from consideration as progressive, then most, if not all, independent progressive schools could not be considered progressive.

- Teachers, as respected professionals, are crucial sources of knowledge about teaching and learning.

As Chapter 8 demonstrated, talented and creative teachers have always been an important part of Dalton's tradition. Teachers at Dalton always were instrumental in constructing curriculum and designing instructional methods. Although teachers today still have significant input into curriculum design and implementation, far more than in most public schools, there has been a not so subtle shift in the place of teachers at Dalton since the Barr administration. As the school grew in size, and with the more rational bureaucratic processes instituted by Dunnan, control of curriculum and instruction increasingly shifted to department chairs, curriculum coordinators, divisional directors, and to the Associate Headmaster, Frank Moretti, who originally was hired as the Assistant Headmaster in charge of Curriculum. Many teachers at Dalton today feel less professionally empowered and appreciated than they did in the past. This seems especially true of veteran teachers who came to Dalton under Durham, Kittell, and to some degree, Barr.

> • Curriculum balance is maintained by commitment to children's individual interests and developmental needs, as well as a commitment to community within and beyond the school's walls.

Historically, the Dalton School always had an explicit commitment to the needs and interests of its students, as well as to the community within and beyond its walls. Founded in the spirit of child-centered pedagogy and Dewey's notion of an embryonic community, Dalton was, and to some extent, still is this kind of school. This is especially true in the First Program and Middle School, less so in the High School, where achievement and college admissions mania sometimes overshadow progressive concerns with the individual. In terms of commitment to the community within and outside, Dalton has a rich tradition in both areas; a tradition that has waned, but not disappeared. During the Parkhurst and Durham administrations a family type atmosphere prevailed. Dalton was a "motherly" institution embracing a philosophy that stressed connections to the community. As many alumni/ae sent their children to Dalton an intergenerational tradition that linked family to school often prevailed. As the school became larger under Barr, and because Barr often discouraged acceptance of alumni/ae children, this community atmosphere began to change. Under Dunnan, the school continued to grow and thus the intimate community of Dalton's past became less tenable. There is still considerable devotion to community, except given its size, it is more difficult. With regard to community service, although it lapsed during Barr's administration, it has been reinstated under Dunnan. While some students believe service to the community is a hollow ritual, it nonetheless remains an important feature of the school's progressive past.

> ● Schools embrace the home cultures of children and their families. Classroom practices reflect these values and bring multiple cultural perspectives to bear.

This is another of the principles attuned to a more diverse school setting. Perhaps one of the problems at Dalton is that it has too closely mirrored the affluent community in which it is located, rather than successfully challenging the values of materialism and affluence. Throughout its history, Dalton has attempted to instill in its students a social conscience; it continues to try to so. As Chapter 9 demonstrated, the values of achievement and success too often dominate.

> ● Students are active constructors of knowledge and learn through direct experience and primary sources.

Historically, this was true at all levels of the Dalton School. Students were always actively engaged in their own learning and progressive experiments such as the Otis Farm trip exemplified experiential education. Today, this is less true, although students at Dalton are probably more involved in their own learning than students at most traditional schools. As the school increased instructional periods and decreased Lab time, traditional instructional practices have become more widespread. In the First Program and the Middle School there is more opportunity for these types of student centered experiences. In the High School, where traditional subject matter is taught in a structured setting and where traditional learning outcomes are stressed, progressive practices are less in evidence.

> ● All disciplines—the arts, sciences, humanities, and physical development—are valued equally in an interdisciplinary curriculum.

Historically, Dalton stressed an interdisciplinary curriculum. This is still in evidence in the First Program, less so in the Middle School and the High School. Although attempts are still made to teach courses which bridge several disciplines, nevertheless, the main thrust of the curriculum is more discipline centered than interdisciplinary. Under the direction of Frank Moretti there has been an attempt to reverse this trend.

> ● Decision making within schools is inclusive of children, parents, and staff.

Historically, school based management and other forms of democratic education never truly existed at the Dalton School. Despite the rhetoric of Deweyan democracy, Helen Parkhurst was an authoritarian leader. Charlotte Durham, although more respectful of her faculty and students, still made the major decisions. Donald Barr ruled by ukase. After his resignation, teachers opposed his being considered as a candidate for Headmaster primarily because of his authoritarian practices. Gardner Dunnan, although much less outwardly dictatorial, nonetheless, has the final say in most policy matters. While teachers and parents have always had a voice, this has been far more one of recommendation, rather than implementation.

> ● The school is a model of democracy and humane relationships confronting issues of racism, classism, and sexism.

Although Dalton has always philosophically confronted issues of racism, classism, and sexism, it is difficult to argue that a school that serves primarily advantaged white children can be held up as a paradigm for progressive concerns of this type. Again, it may be unfair to judge the school in this manner given its population, nonetheless, it cannot be termed a model of democracy in action. The history of leadership at Dalton, from Parkhurst to Dunnan, suggests that democratic education has been difficult to implement.

> ● Schools actively support critical inquiry into the complexities of global issues. Children can thus assume the powerful responsibilities of world citizenship.

Historically, this has been a hallmark of a Dalton education and continues to be so. Students actively participate in political, environmental, social, and community activities and the curriculum is concerned with social problems. In many respects, a Dalton education has always attempted to prepare its students for assuming responsibility along the line envisioned by Dewey in his writings on democracy and education.

* * *

This analysis suggests that progressive principles have not been abandoned entirely at Dalton. It does, however, indicate that the school is not very progressive by these contemporary standards. It is an elite, competitive school, which attempts where possible to be true to its progressive heritage and does so inconsistently. Where it is most successful is in terms of progressive pedagogic practices, such as interdisciplinary curriculum and child-centered pedagogy. Where it is least successful is in terms of democratic education and its over-emphasis on achievement.

I began this chapter by asking whether or not the transformation was both necessary and inevitable. Or to what degree could the school have maintained its progressive practices more fully? As more histories of progressive schools are written, perhaps we will be in a better position to respond with a degree of certainty. This history of the Dalton School cannot definitively answer these questions. Any answer on my part would be more speculative than historically sound and would be rooted in my own subjective experiences at Dalton. The history of the school demonstrates what a school did to survive in an increasingly competitive and market driven independent school world. That I wish it had remained more progressive is certainly true; I have no illusions that this would necessarily have been possible. Despite these changes, the Dalton School has always been and continues to be a special place. It is just not as progressive as it once was. Hopefully, as the histories of other progressive schools are written, we will be in a better position to understand how and why progressive schools change and to be better able to help them preserve their heritages.

BIBLIOGRAPHY

Conversations with the Following People

Wayne Adamson
Mary Alexander
Ann Arnold
David Arnold
Richard Bader, M.D.
Jan Barnet
Donald Barr
Thelma Blackburn
Alan Boyers
Constance Mayer Boyers
Andrea Bromley
Theresa Bruno
Susan Buksbaum
Linda Bunting
Benjamin Buttenwieser
Frank Carnabuci
Betty Chapin
Ellen Cohen
James Cohen
Carol Cone
Peter W. Cookson, Jr.
Susan Cookson
Winthrop Crane
David Cremin
Lawrence A. Cremin
Mary diCarlo
Scott Diddell
James Dinerman
Jeffrey Dryfoos
Gardner Dunnan

Charlotte Durham
Susan Etess
Jeanne Ernst
Graziella España
Audrey Feuerstein
Charles Fisher
Lucille Fleschner
Jamie Gangel
Elizabeth Garn
Judy Geller
Zelda Gitlin
Roz Glantz
Lloyd Goodrich
Patricia Graham
Louisa Gralla
Janet Greene
Carol Hammer
Ellen Harteveldt
Cameron Hendershot
Margo Hentoff
Nora Hodges
Philip Jackson
Kathe Jervis
Rosemarie Keller
Rita Kramer
Aaron Kurzen
Robert LaHoten
Arlene Landesman
Robert Machinist
Richard Malenky
Joanna Marcus
Mary Marshall
Frank Moretti
Marilyn Moss
Milton Mound
Isabelle Mound
Chester Page
Rhea Paige

Greg Palitz
Alvin Parkhurst
Paul Poet
Marjorie Pleshette
Gerda Prokuda
Richard Ravitch
Georgia Rice
Susan Rolfe
Rona Roob
Edmund Rosenthal
Tessie Ross
Royce Roth
Sandra Schwabacher
Stanley Seidman
Nell Semel
David Sidorsky
Gordon Smith
Judy Stecher
Judy Steckler
Rebecca Straus
Ralph Tyler
Hortense Tyroler
Dietrich von Bothmer

Correspondence

Charlotte Durham
Trudy Pratt
Ralph Tyler

Unpublished Materials in the Dalton Archives

Assignments from Donald Barr through Gardner Dunnan.

Articles by Helen Parkhurst.

Biography of Helen Parkhurst by Marilyn Feldman, School Archivist and Librarian.

Eight Year Experience: Dalton School, 1940.

Evaluation by Donald Barr, 1974.

Faculty Handbooks from Donald Barr through Gardner Dunnan.

Faculty Meeting Minutes, "Philosophy and Objectives," February 21-22, 1940.

Pamphlets (incomplete) from Donald Barr through Gardner Dunnan issued by the Admissions Office.

Publicity File in the Archives containing articles on Dalton from 1960 on from *Newsweek, Time, Penthouse,* etc.

Student Publications: *Blue Flag* (from 1940-incomplete); *Daltonian* (1936-59; 1967-91).

Headmaster's Archives

Atkins, Thurston and Barth, Roland. Outside Reviews of the Middle School Program of the Dalton School, December, 1979.

Evaluations mandated by the Board, 1974: John Jones, Philip Jackson, Ralph Tyler.

Minutes of the Board of Trustees from Helen Parkhurst through Gardner Dunnan beginning in 1929.

New York State Association of Independent Schools (NYSIAS) Report of the Visiting Committee, March, 1984.

New York State Association of Independent Schools (NYSIAS) Report of the Visiting Committee, March, 1985.

New York State Association of Independent Schools (NYSIAS) Report of
the Visiting Committee, June, 1986

Self-Evaluation of the First Program, December, 1983.

Self-Evaluation of the Middle School, February, 1985.

Self-Evaluation of the High School, March, 1986.

The Transition Committee. End of Year Report, April 1982.

Books

Aiken, Wilford M. *The Story of the Eight Year Study*. Cambridge, MA and
London: Harvard University Press, 1980.

Antler, Joyce. *Lucy Sprague Mitchell: The Making of a Modern Woman*.
New Haven: Yale University Press, 1987.

Barr, Donald. *Who Pushed Humpty Dumpty?* New York: Atheneum, 1971.

Bell, Bernard Iddings. *Crisis in Education*. New York: Whittlesey House,
1949.

Bernstein, Basil. *Class, Codes and Control, Vol. 1*. London: Routledge,
1973.

____. *Class, Codes and Control, Vol. 3*. London: Routledge, 1975.

____. *The Structuring of Pedagogic Discourse, Class, Codes and Control,
Vol. 4*. London: Routledge, 1990.

Bestor, Arthur. *Educational Wastelands*. Urbana: University of Illinois
Press, 1953.

Blumberg, Antler and Greenfield, William D. *The Effective Principal:
Perspectives on School Leadership*. Boston: Allyn and Bacon,
1980.

Bruner, Jerome. *The Process of Education*. Cambridge, MA: Harvard University Press, 1960.

Callahan, Raymond. *Education and the Cult of Efficiency*. Chicago: University of Chicago Press, 1962.

Chubb, John and Moe, Terry. *Politics, Markets, and Schools*. Washington, D.C.: The Brookings Institute, 1990.

Coleman, James S. et al. *Equality of Educational Opportunity*. Washington, D.C.: Government Printing Office, 1966.

Coleman, James; Hoffer, Thomas and Kilgore, Sally. *Public and Private Schools*. Washington, D.C.: National Center for Educational Statistics, 1981.

_____. *High School Achievement: Public, Catholic, and Private Schools Compared*. New York: Basic Books, 1982.

Collins, Randall. *The Credential Society*. New York: Acacemic Press, 1979.

Collins, Randall and Makowsky, Michael. *The Discovery of Society*. New York: Random House, 1978.

Cookson, Peter W. Jr. and Persell, Caroline Hodges. *Preparing for Power: America's Elite Boarding Schools*. New York: Basic Books, 1985.

Cookson, Peter, W. Jr.; Sadovnik, Alan R. and Semel, Susan F. *International Hanbook of Educational Reform*. Westport, CT: Greenwood Press, 1992.

Cremin, Lawrence A. *The Transformation of the School*. New York: Alfred A. Knopf and Random House, 1961.

_____. *The Genius of American Education*. New York: Alfred A. Knopf and Random House, 1965.

_____. *American Education: The Metropolitan Experience*. New York: Harper and Row, 1988.

_____. *Popular Education and its Discontents*. New York: Harper and Row, 1990.

Cuban, Larry. *How Teachers Taught: Constancy and Change in American Classrooms,1890- 1980*. New York: Longman, 1984.

Curti, Merle E. *The Social Ideas of American Educators*. New York: Charles Scribner's Sons, 1935.

Dewey, Evelyn. *The Dalton Laboratory Plan*. New York: E.P. Dutton and Co. 1922.

Dewey, John. *Experience and Education*. New York: Macmillan, 1938.

_____. *The Child and the Curriculum* and *The School and Society*. Chicago: University of Chicago Press, 1956. (Combined ed.)

_____. *My Pedagogic Creed*. In Martin S. Dworkin, ed. *Dewey on Education: Selections*. New York: Teachers College Press, 1959. pp. 19-32.

Dewey, John, and Dewey, Evelyn. *Schools of To-Morrow*. New York: E.P. Dutton and Co., 1915.

Dickstein, Morris. *Gates of Eden*. New York: Basic Book, 1977.

Douglas, Jack. *Investigative Social Research*. Newburg Park, CA: Sage Publications, 1972.

Dykhuizen, George. *The Life and Mind of John Dewey*. Carbondale and Edwardsville: Southern Illinois University Press, 1973.

Dworkin, Martin. *Dewey on Education: Selections*. New York: Teachers College Press, 1959.

Featherstone, Joseph. *Schools Where Children Learn*. New York: Liveright, 1971.

Feldman, Marilyn Moss, ed. *Dalton School, A Book of Memories*. New York: Dalton School, 1979.

Freire, Paulo. *Pedagogy of the Oppressed*. New York: Herder and Herder, 1971.

Freedman, Samuel G. *Small Victories*. New York: Harper and Row, 1990.

Fullan, Michael. *The Meaning of Educational Change*. New York: Teachers College Press, 1981.

Gardner, Howard. *Frames of Mind: A Theory of Multiple Intelligences*. New York: Basic Books, 1983.

Geer, Amanda Katie. *The Progressive Origins of The Putney School, Examined Through the Life of Carmelita Chase Hinton*. Putney, VT: The Putney School, 1982.

Giles, H. H., McCutchen, S. P., and Zechiel, A. N. *Exploring the Curriculum*. New York and London: Harper and Brothers, 1942.

Goldman, Eric. *The Crucial Decade—And After*. New York: Random House, 1960.

Graham, Patricia Albjerg, *Progressive Education: From Arcady to Academe*. New York, Teachers College Press, 1967.

Grant, Gerald. *The World We Created at Hamilton High*. Cambridge: Harvard University Press, 1988.

Graubard, Allen. *Free the Children: Radical Reform and the Free School Movement*. New York: Random House, 1972.

Greene, Maxine. *Teacher As Stranger*. Belmont, Cal.: Wadsworth Publishing Co., 1973.

_____. *Landscapes of Learning*. New York: Teachers College Press, 1978.

_____. *The Dialectic of Freedom*. New York: Teachers College Press, 1988.

Hainstock, Elizabeth. *The Essential Montessori*. New York: New American Library, 1978.

Hampel, Robert L. *The Last Little Citadel: American High Schools Since 1940*. Boston: Houghton Mifflin Company, 1986.

Heirich, Max. *Berkeley*. New York: Columbia University Press, 1968-1970.

Hofstadter, Richard. *Anti-intellectualism in American Life*. New York: Vintage Books, 1962-1963.

Ianni, Francis A. J. *Conflict and Change in Education*. Glenview, ILL.: Scott, Foresman, 1975.

Ianni, Francis A. J. and Reuss-Ianni, Elizabeth. *A Family Business*. New York: Russell Sage Foundation, 1972.

Jaffe, Rona. *Class Reunion*. New York: Delacorte Press, 1979.

Jencks, Christopher, and Riesman, David. *The Academic Revolution*. Garden City, N.Y.: Doubleday, 1968.

Jencks, Christopher, et al. *Inequality: A Reassessment of the Effect of Family and Schooling in America*. New York: Basic Books, 1972.

Jervis, Kathe and Montag, Carol, eds. *Progressive Education for the 1990s*. New York: Teachers College Press, 1991.

Karier, Clarence J., Violas, Paul C., and Spring, Joel. *Roots of Crisis: American Education in the Twentieth Century*. Chicago: Rand-McNally, 1973.

Katz, Michael B. *Class, Bureaucracy and Schools*. New York: Praeger,

1971.

_____. *Reconstructing American Education*. Cambridge: Harvard University Press,' 1987.

Kavanaugh, Robert. *The Grim Generation*. New York: Trident Press, 1970.

Kimmins, C.W. and Rennie, Belle. *The Triumph of the Dalton Plan*. London: Nicholson and Watson, 1923.

Kohl, Herbert. *36 Children*. New York: New American Library, 1967.

Kozol, Jonathan. *Death at an Early Age*. New York: New American Library, 1965.

Kraushaar, Otto F. *American Nonpublic Schools: Patterns of Diversity*. Baltimore and London: Johns Hopkins University Press, 1972.

Lareau, Annette. *Home Advantage*. London: Falmer Press, 1989.

Lebarle, Marc, and Seligson, Tom. *The High School Revolutionaries*. New York: Random House, 1970.

Leichter, Hope Jensen, ed. *The Family as Educator*. New York: Teachers College Press, 1975.

Lepham, James and Hoeh, James A. *The Principalship: Foundations and Functions*. New York: Harper and Row, 1974.

Lightfoot, Sara Lawrence. *The Good High School*. New York: Basic Books, 1983.

Lloyd, Susan M. *The Putney School: A Progressive Experiment*. New Haven: Yale University Press, 1987.

Lynch, A.J. *Individual Work and the Dalton Plan*. London: George Philip and Son, 1924.

_____. *The Rise and Progress of the Dalton Plan*. London: George Philip and Son, 1926.

Marcus, Robert D., and Bruner, David, eds. *America Since 1945*. New York: St. Martin's Press, 1977.

Montessori, Maria. *The Montessori Method*. New York: Frederick A. Stokes Co., 1912.

Neill, A.S. *Summerhill: A Radical Approach to Child Rearing*. New York: Hart, 1960.

Newman, Joseph W. *America's Teachers: An Introduction to Education*. New York: Longman, 1990.

O'Neill, William J. *Coming Apart: An Informal History of America in the 1960s*. Chicago: Quadrangle Books, 1971.

Parker, Francis W. *Talks on Teaching*. New York: E.L. Kellogg and Co., 1903.

_____. *Talks on Pedagogics*. New York: A.S. Barnes & Co., 1984.

Parkhurst, Helen. *Education on the Dalton Plan*. London: G. Bell and Sons, 1927.

Patterson, James T. *America in the Twentieth Century*. New York: Harcourt Brace Jovanovich, 1976.

Perrow, Charles. *Complex Organizations*. 2nd ed. Glenview, Ill.: Scott, Foresman, 1979.

Peters, Thomas J., and Waterman, Robert H., Jr. *In Search of Excellence: Lessons from America's Best-Run Companies*. New York: Harper and Row, 1982.

Powell, Arthur G., Farr, Eleanor and Cohen, David K. *The Shopping Mall High School*. Boston: Houghton Mifflin Company, 1985.

Postman, Neil and Weingartner, Charles. *Teaching as a Subversive Activity*. New York: Dell Publishing Co., Inc. 1969.

Pratt, Caroline. *Experimental Practice in the City and Country School*. New York: E.P. Dutton and Co., 1924.

Ravitch, Diane. *The Troubled Crusade*. New York: Basic Books, 1983.

Rickover, H. G. *Education and Freedom*. New York: E. P. Dutton and Co., 1959.

Rugg, Harold and Schumaker, Ann. *The Child-Centered School*. New York: Arno Press, 1969.

Rutter, Michael; Maughan, Barbara; Mortimore, Peter; Ouston, Janet: Smith and Alan. *Fifteen Thousand Hours: Secondary Schools and Their Effects on Children*. Cambridge: Harvard University Press, 1979.

Sadovnik, Alan R., ed. *Basil Bernstein: Consensus and Controversy*. Norwood, N.J.: Ablex Publishing Corporation, forthcoming.

Sarason, Seymour B. *The Culture of the School and the Problem of Change*. Boston: Allyn and Bacon, 1971.

Seeger, Elizabeth. *The Pageant of Chinese History*. New York: David McKay Co., 1934.

Shakeshaft, Charol. *Women in Educational Administration*. Newburg Park, California: Sage Publications, 1987.

Silberman, Charles. *Crisis in the Classroom*. New York: Random House, 1970.

Sizer, Theodore R. *Horace's Compromise: The Dilemma of the American High School*. Boston: Houghton Mifflin Company, 1984.

Smith, Eugene R.; Tyler, Ralph W.; and The Evaluation Staff. *Appraising and Recording Student Progress*. New York and London: Harper and Brothers, 1942.

Stone, Marie Kirchner, ed. *Between Home and Community: Chronicle of the Francis W. Parker School 1901-1976*. Chicago, Francis W. Parker School, 1976.

Strain, John Paul. *Modern Philosophies of Education*. New York: Random House, 1971.

Swidler, Ann. *Organization Without Authority: Dilemmas of Social Control in Free Schools*. Cambridge, Mass. and London: Harvard University Press, 1979.

Time, Inc. *This Fabulous Century*. Vol. 2. New York: Time-Life Books, 1970.

Tyack, David B. *The One Best System: A History of American Urban Education*. Cambridge, MA and London: Harvard University Press, 1974.

Tyack, David B. and Hansot, Elizabeth. *Managers of Viture: Public School Leadership in America, 1920-1980*. New York: Basic Books, 1982.

____. *Learning Together: A History of Coeducation in American Schools*. New Haven: Yale University Press, 1990.

Vandenberg, Donald. *Being and Education*. Englewood Cliffs, N.J.: Prentice-Hall, 1971.

Washburne, Carlton W. *Adjusting the School to the Child*. New York: World Book Co., 1932.

Washburne, Carlton W., and Marland, Sidney P., Jr. *Winnetka: The History and Significance of an Educational Experiment*. Englewood Cliffs, N. J.: Prentice-Hall, 1963.

Wigginton, Eliot. *Sometimes A Shining Moment: The Forfire Experiment*.

Garden City, New York: Doubleday, 1986.

Yankelovich, Daniel. *Changing Youth Values in the 1970's: A Study of American Youth*. New York: J.D. Rockefeller Foundation, 1974.

Yeomans, Edward, *The Shady Hill School: The First Fifty Years*. Cambridge, Windflower Press, 1979.

Zweigenhaft, Richard L., and Domhoff, G. William. *Jews in the Protestant Establishment*. New York: Praeger, 1982.

_____. *Blacks in the White Establishment?* New Haven: Yale University Press, 1991.

Periodicals and Unpublished Materials
Not in the Archives

Alumni News of the Dalton School. c.1988-1990. In the author's possession.

Barth, Roland and Deal, Terrence E. "The Principalship: Views from Within and Without." *The Effective Principal*. Reston, Virginia: National Association of Secondary School Principals, 1982.

Chubb, John and Moe, Terry. "Political Pollyannas." Teachers College Record, Volume 93, Number 1, 1991, pp. 161-165.

Cookson, Peter W., Jr. "Politics, Markets, and America's Schools: A Review." *Teachers College Record*, Volume 93, Number 1, Fall 1991, pp. 156-160.

"The Dalton Brawl." *Time*, April 5, 1971, pp. 44-45.

The Daltonian. c.1980-1991. In author's possession.

The Dalton School Annual Report. c.1988-1991. In the author's possession.

Deffenbaugh, W. S. "Let the Children Advance According to Individual Ability." *School Life* 10 January 1925, pp. 97-98.

Devlin, Peter. "In Search of a Stronger Positive Ethos." Paper submitted for "Foundations of Secondary Education", Fall, 1991 at Adelphi University, Garden City, New York.

Edmonds, Ronald R. "Some Schools Work and More Can." Social Policy, March-April, 1979, pp. 28-32.

Edwards, June. "To Teach Responsibility, Bring Back the Dalton Plan." *Phi Delta Kappan* 72 January, 1991, pp. 398-401.

Former VW-SP teacher honored at dedication," *Stevens Point (WISC) Daily Journal*, March 4, 1974.

Fiedler, Meredith. "College—The C-Word" Submitted for an English course, the Dalton School, New York City, Spring, 1988.

Gibbon, Peter Hazen. "Hartwick: Portrait of an Independent School." Ph.D. dissertation, Columbia University, 1980.

Greenfield, William D. "Research on School Principals: An Analysis." *The Effective Principal.* Reston, Virginia: National Association of Secondary School Principals, 1983.

Gross, Beatrice and Gross, Ronald. "A Little Bit of Chaos." *Saturday Review*, May 16, 1970.

Hechinger, Fred. "Gift of a Great Teacher." *New York Times, November 10, 1987.*

"He's a Hip Headmaster." *New York Post*, October 17, 1973.

Jackman, E. D. "The Dalton Plan." *School Review* 28 November, 1920, pp. 688-96.

Johnson, F. W. "The Dalton Plan." *Teachers College Record* 16 February

1925, pp. 464-72.

Kaestle, Carl F. "The Public Schools and the Public Mood." *American Heritage*, February 1990, pp. 66-81.

Kanner, Bernice. "The Admissions Go-Round: Private School Fever". *New York Magazine*, November 23, 1987, pp. 40-47.

Meyer, John W. and Rowen, Brian. "Institutionalized Organizations: Formal Structure as Myth and Ceremony." *American Journal of Sociology,* September, 1977.

Parker, Franklin, "Ideas That Shaped American Schools." *Phi Delta Kappan* Volume 62, January 1981, pp. 314-19.

Persell, Caroline Hodges and Cookson, Peter W., Jr. "The Effective Principal in Action." *The Effective Principal.* Reston, Virginia: National Association of Secondary School Principals, 1983.

Sadovnik, Alan R. "Basil Bernstein's Theory of Pedagogic Practice: A Structuralist Approach." *Sociology of Education*, Volume 64, January 1991, pp.48-63.

Semel, Susan F. "Bernstein and the History of American Education." In Alan R. Sadovnik, *Basil Bernstein: Consensus and Controversy.* Norwood, N.J.: Ablex Publishing Corporation, forthcoming.

Schickel, Richard. "Traffic Jam in the Private Schools." *New York Times Magazine*, March 12, 1967, pp. 26-27.

Schumer, Fran. "Dalton, Class of 1978". *7 Days*, January 4, 1989, pp. 29-35.

Sopkin, Charles; Tetlow, Carin; and McCalmont, Lucretia. "The Parents' Revolt at Dalton: The Worst Is Yet to Come." *New York Magazine*, May 10, 1971, p. 50.

Wells, Amy Stuart. "Choice in Education: Examining the Evidence on

Equity." *Teachers College Record*, Volume 93, Number 1, 1991, pp. 138-155.

Yuki, Gary. "Managerial Leadership and the Effective Principal." *The Effective Principal*. Reston, Virginia: National Association of Secondary School Principals, 1982.

INDEX